D0237534

**Picture Composition for
Film and Television**

'07

However faithful an image that serves to convey visual information may be, the process of selection will always reveal the maker's interpretation of what he considers relevant.

E.H. Gombrich, *The Image and the Eye*

Picture Composition for Film and Television

Peter Ward

Focal Press
An imprint of Butterworth–Heinemann Ltd
Linacre House, Jordan Hill, Oxford OX2 8DP

$\mathcal{R}$ A member of the Reed Elsevier plc group

OXFORD LONDON BOSTON
MUNICH NEW DELHI SINGAPORE SYDNEY
TOKYO TORONTO WELLINGTON

First published 1996

British Library Cataloguing in Publication Data
Ward, Peter
  Picture Composition for Film and Television
  Television
  I. Title
  778.53

ISBN 0240 51421 1

Library of Congress Cataloguing in Publication Data
A catalogue record for this book is available from
the Library of Congress.

Composition by Scribe Design, Gillingham, Kent
Printed in Great Britain

Contents

Preface

In the last years of the nineteenth century, moving pictures were viewed in penny arcades on Thomas Edison's Kinetoscope. The solo viewer cranked a handle, peered into a darkened box and was fascinated by the dim flickering representations of movement. This was quickly supplanted by projected images but the mystery of a miniature world continued to have a strong attraction. After nearly forty years as a cameraman, I am still intrigued by a similar magic whenever I look through a viewfinder. There is a concentration of the field of view into a small intense, two-dimensional image which is quite unlike normal perception.

Moving the camera, lens and viewpoint creates a continuing kaleidoscope of changing images. Some images are attractive and pleasing whilst others are dull frames, a confused slice of passing reality. What makes the difference? What is the distinction between an image on the screen that delights the eye and the everyday, depiction of a commonplace 'window' on the world?

It may be the content of the picture that fixes the attention or it may be the technical quality of the image that is enjoyed. Frequently, however, it is the often unconscious pleasure derived from an arrangement of mass, line, tone and colour. The composition of the image appears to be one aspect of film and television production that attracts the audience and holds their attention.

 Composition – the arrangement of all the visual elements within the frame, is at the heart of all visual communication. It is a subject that is seldom taught to broadcasting/film trainees who are expected to learn by example or to fall back on intuition or instinct. Many cameramen in fact, insist that composition is intuitive and assume that framing decisions are based on personal and subjective opinion. Even a cursory examination of an evening's output of television will demonstrate the near uniformity of standard conventions in composition. There are original and innovative exceptions and this book aims to discuss the differences and the conventions of picture composition.

Throughout the book I use the term 'cameraman' without wishing to imply that this craft is restricted to one gender. 'Cameraman' is the customary title to describe a job which is practised by both men and women and 'he', where it occurs, should be read as 'he/she'.

My thanks to Robert Kruger, Alan Bermingham, Nick Viliesid, Keith Salmon and Nick Collier for reading the manuscript and making many helpful and constructive suggestions. Needless to say, any errors or omissions in the book are mine. My thanks also to Mary Beresford-Williams for permission to reprint her photographs of television production. A special thanks to Patrick Caulfield for providing the drawing for the frontispiece of the book and to my wife, Sue, and my children, Sally and Edmund, for their help and encouragement in its production.

The cover picture is from 'The Big Combo' from the film library of Richard L. Rosenfeld, whose permission to reproduce it is gratefully acknowledged.

1

Introduction

What is composition?

Composition is commonly defined as arranging all the visual elements in the frame in a way that makes the image a satisfactory and a complete whole. Integration of the image is obtained by the positioning of line, mass, colour and light in the most pleasing arrangement.

This definition is a start in the examination of composition but it does prompt further questions. What counts as 'satisfactory and complete' and is 'pleasing arrangement' an objective or subjective judgement?

The definition also has a half-hidden assumption that the purpose of pictorial composition is always to provide an agreeable visual experience independent of the purpose of the shot. Film and TV productions obviously serve more purposes than simply providing a 'pleasing arrangement' of images. There appears to be other aspects of picture making to be examined before answering the question – what is good composition and what function does it serve?

This book will concentrate on how to arrange a given subject for maximum visual effect. The subject of the shot is the predominantly influential element but many cameramen, in devising solutions to visual problems (another definition of composition) have to work with a subject that has already been selected. The cameraman's role usually centres on deciding between a choice of techniques on how best to handle the given material. In everyday programme production, there may be opportunities for the cameraman to select material that provides good visual potential but frequently the subject is prescribed by script or brief and the cameraman has to devise the best shot that can be achieved with the available material.

Whether the composition of any photographic image has succeeded could be judged by a number of criteria. The chapter on perception looks at the way images attract and hold attention and the relationship between the nature of human perception and how visual elements can be grouped and arranged to maintain interest.

Figure 1.1

Perspective, the influence of the frame and the visual design elements available to the cameraman are discussed in relation to defining the purpose of a shot, creating and controlling visual elements to facilitate the transmission of the intended message and what is needed to create and control the image to establish atmosphere. Does the image convey, by its presentation, the reason why the shot was recorded?

Light, colour, how action is staged and camera movement all influence decisions about composition but they are never self-contained elements in the final image. A dynamic forceful image is not adequately analysed by identifying the constituent parts and a shot never exists in isolation. Answers to questions such as – is the image relevant to its context, what is the relationship to the previous and succeeding shots, what are the visual style and conventions of the programme genre and what is the influence of current fashions and styles, all contribute to the structure of the composition.

There are many factors at work when framing up a shot and in describing the general principles that influence compositional decisions there is a need to set the current working practices and visual conventions in some sort of context. How and why did these conventions arise? The chapter on past influences looks mainly at the Hollywood film tradition of 'invisible technique'.

This technique grew out of the need for unobtrusive shot transition and camera movement on shot in order to achieve a seamless flow of images in the story telling. A number of 'invisible' techniques were discovered and became the standard conventions of film making and later television camerawork.

In essence this convention directs the audience attention to the action rather than the mechanics of production. Methods are employed to cut between shots, to keep attention on what is contained within the frame rather than beyond its enclosing area and to move the camera smoothly on shot to a new viewpoint without distracting the audience.

There are other conventions of presentation which intentionally draw attention to the means of production. Camera movement in this alternative technique is often restlessly on the move, panning abruptly from subject to subject, making no effort to disguise the transitions and deliberately drawing attention to the means by which the images are brought to the viewer. This breaking down or subverting the Hollywood convention of an 'invisible' seamless flow of images has a number of different forms or styles which require a separate treatment.

As there is this emphasis on the 'Hollywood' model of 'invisible technique' of image making in mass entertainment and the majority of cameramen work within this convention, it would seem appropriate that it should be thoroughly understood and described. This analysis does not necessarily endorse these conventions over any other method of production but simply seeks to explain the principles of the techniques employed.

Composition involves a number of factors which at times interact and overlap. In attempting to tease out and describe constituent elements there is often the need to look again at basic compositional requirements by way of a new visual design. Pictorial unity is achieved by integrating all the visual elements within a frame but in attempting to describe the constituent parts it has not always been possible to keep these topics separated in watertight chapters.

Intuition

It is the folklore of film and TV cameramen that composition is intuitive and therefore almost inexplicable. Whereas trainees and juniors on camera crews have access to volumes of technical explanation about exposure, film stock, electronic image making and all the other technical descriptions of the tools of their trade, composition – the heart of visual communication, is considered a God-given talent that is either understood, or if it is not, then the unfortunate individual who lacks compositional ability is seen to be similar to a tone deaf person and would not know good composition if it jumped out of the viewfinder and hit him in the eye.

Johannes Itten, an art teacher, gave this advice to his students

If you, unknowing, are able to create masterpieces in colour, then unknowledge is your way. But if you are unable to create masterpieces in colour out of your unknowledge, then you ought to look for knowledge.

Many of us working in film and TV know, through many years of experience, exactly how to reposition the lens in space or choose a different lens-angle in order to improve the appearance of the shot. We are either working to inherited craft values of what is 'good' composition or we are repositioning and juggling with the camera until we intuitively feel that we have solved that particular visual problem. Frequently there is no time to analyse a situation and the only thing to fall back on is experience. Compositional experience is the result of many years of solving visual problems. Good visual communication is not a gift from heaven but is learnt from finding out in practice what does and does not work.

The following chapters attempt to review and reveal why certain visual solutions to framing are considered acceptable and where and how these standards originated and developed. There are aspects of composition that are subjective and determined by individual taste but much of what is considered standard practice both in painting and in the creation of film and television images is conditioned by the innate requirements of human perception.

'I see what you mean!'

There is usually a reason why a shot is recorded on tape or film.The purpose may be simply to record an event or the image may play an important part in expressing a complex idea. Whatever the reasons that initiate the shot, the cameraman recording the shot should have an understanding of compositional technique if the idea to be expressed is to be clearly communicated to the intended audience.

The appearance as well as the content of the shot is an integral part in the process of communication. Often, as in painting, form and content of screen images are inseparable. It is accepted that in a drama production the composition of the shot will play a major part in the storytelling. The form, as well the content of the shot, is used to tell the story. But even in the hardest of 'hard news' stories where objectivity is striven for and the camera is intended to be a neutral observer, the effect of the image on the audience will depend on camera framing and camera position. Each time the record button is pressed, a number of crucial decisions affecting clear communication have been consciously or unconsciously made.

The development of photography in the nineteenth century was considered by many people as a new and objective way of recording the real world, unhampered by the subjective mediation of the individual artist. It was some time before people realized that the camera was as partial in the image it produces as a painter. Whenever a camera converts a three-dimensional subject into a two-dimensional picture the imprint of the lens height, camera tilt, distance from subject and lens-angle is present in the composition of the shot.

The cameraman therefore needs to understand all the elements of visual design if he is to convey precisely the idea or event that is intended to be communicated. If he or she ignores conscious compositional decisions, then 'auto composition' takes over and by default, the camera provides images which are a product of the characteristics of the camera and lens rather than the manipulator of the camera.

Visual imagery has its own version of grammar and syntax which requires the same discernment and application to achieve precise communication as that practised in the study of language.

Why composition is important

A cameraman shows the audience where to look. His role is to solve visual problems usually in the shortest possible time. Although the cameraman's presence in factual programme making can influence or disrupt the subject matter, the bottom line is to get the best possible rendering of what is there.

An image should communicate in a simple, direct way and not have to rely on a 'voice-over' to explain, reveal or argue its significance. The definitive shot has the relevant content with all the visual elements in the frame organized to achieve clear communication. Audio 'atmosphere' and effects will reinforce the message that is communicated but often the compositional design will condition how the image is perceived. There must be no confusion in the viewer's mind about the purpose for which the shot was taken.

Good composition reinforces the manner in which the mind organizes information. It emphasizes those elements such as grouping, pattern, shape and form that provide the viewer with the best method of 'reading' the image smoothly and efficiently. If there is friction in visual movement of the eye across the frame, if there are areas of the image which stop the eye dead, then an unsatisfactory feeling is unconsciously experienced and in an extreme form will end the attention of the viewer. There is a fine dividing line between 'teasing' the eye with visual ambiguities and losing the interest of the audience.

The cameraman must help the viewer to perceive what is intended to be communicated by providing design guidelines to channel the movement of the eye within the frame. The eye movement must be continuous and smooth and be led in a premeditated route across the relevant parts of the subject matter without any distracting detours to unimportant visual elements in the frame. It is part of the cameraman's craft to create shots that are well designed and engage the attention of the viewer. Simply putting a frame around a subject by a 'point and shoot' technique will often result in incoherent visual design that fails to connect.

The image produced by a camera has no memory, knowledge or experience of the content. If you, as the cameraman, have additional details about the subject which are not contained within the frame but which would help you to understand the image, the audience will also need that knowledge or it will supply its own conjectures. If this extra knowledge is vital to the information that is intended to be conveyed, the shot is incomplete and partial communication only can be achieved. You must consider whether the image can explain all that is required without additional explanation.

Control of composition

Control of composition is achieved by the ability to choose the appropriate camera technique such as viewpoint, focal length of lens, lighting, exposure in addition to employing a range of visual design elements such as balance, colour contrast, perspective of mass/line, etc.

A well-designed composition is one in which the visual elements have either been selectively included or excluded. The visual components of the composition must be organized to engage the viewer's attention. A starting point is often to follow the old advice to simplify by elimination, and to reduce to essentials in order to create an image that has strength and clarity.

Visual design techniques

Much of the technique employed in programme/film production is the result of subjective decisions chosen from a range of possible options in sympathy with the main narrative or programme requirements. Alongside subjective creative preferences there are also objective principles of design and specific ways of organizing the image to have predictable effects. Good visual design involves elements of individual creativity plus a knowledge of the role of a number of factors that affect the way an image is perceived. These will be dealt with in detail in the appropriate chapter and include light, figure/ground relationship, shape, frame, balance, light/dark relationships, line, perspective of mass and line, colour, content.

Cultural influences

Some aspects of compositional technique are timeless whilst others are fashionably of the moment. They both have a part to play in the well-designed shot. The image should be designed to satisfy an aesthetic appreciation as well as the quest for information. This aesthetic 'buzz' changes with culture and fashion over time. Attention can be captured by the new and the novel but when dealing with a mass audience, attention can just as easily be lost if current conventions and the expectations of the audience are flouted and the shock of the new is used with the mistaken idea of grabbing attention. As will be seen in the psychology of perception, people ignore what they cannot understand. Communication can only be achieved if you have the attention of the audience.

Changing fashion

Figure 1.2 The 'over-the-shoulder two shot' was first used in about 1910. It still appears in the majority of narrative films.

Styles of film and TV camerawork change but the stylistic changes are usually elements of narrative presentation rather than in compositional form. Barry Salt in *Film Style and Technology* identified the first use of the 'over-the-shoulder two shot' in about 1910. The reverse angle shot of faces inter-cut in dialogue appeared in 'The Loafer' (a silent western) in 1912. These basic compositional techniques have become part of the language of visual storytelling. Shot structures are refashioned, editing conventions in the presentation of time and space are re-worked, conventions of narrative continuity are challenged and replaced but many composition conventions have remained (Figure 2.1).

Such compositional conventions are considered normal or standard and have been learnt over time by cinema-goers and TV viewers. These compositional stereotypes can be reinforced or confronted. Human perception functions by seeking to simplify complex forms and patterns but this can be frustrated by the cameraman if, in his choice of framing, he creates disorganized images. 'But what is it?', the viewer inquires when presented with an unfamiliar image. The search to classify is natural to the human mind and a perceptual 'puzzle' may engage the attention of an observer up to the point where he or she gives up the attempt to decode its significance. This point will vary with the individual but many people, anticipating a familiar and recognizable image on the screen, have an aversion to the unfamiliar. If the shot cannot immediately be categorized, they may mentally switch off if their image of visual reality is too severely challenged.

But visual storytelling will often demand puzzling or challenging images in order to create mystery or suspense. Keeping the audience guessing is a well-used visual convention in narrative film making. The American cinematographer William Fraker was setting up a shot for 'Rosemary's Baby'. The director Roman Polanski requested a specific framing through a door to show a woman telephoning in the adjacent room but had so placed the camera that the woman's face was masked by the door frame. Fraker wanted to reposition the camera to bring the face into view, Polanski resisted. 'With my framing,' he explained, 'we will have every member of the audience craning to their right in an attempt to see the face behind the doorframe.' The function of this shot was to withhold information in order to feed the curiosity of the audience in the development of the story.

Summary

In summary, good composition is the best arrangement of the subject matter in sympathy with the function of the shot. It should have simplicity and intensity and achieve its objective with clarity, precision and economy.

2
Perception

Perception

There is not much point in talking to someone unless they are listening. The first function of composition must be to capture the attention of the audience.

Effective communication can be carried out in many languages. The very basic requirement for communication between individuals is their need to speak in the same language. Using a visual medium is choosing to communicate through pictures and ultimately the visual language used must be compatible with human perception. Although aesthetic fashion influences composition, good visual communication rests on an understanding of the psychology of perception.

Man has specific ways of visually understanding the world. If a composition is arranged to work in accord with those underlying visual principles, then there is more chance of the visual information being understood and enjoyed. If the composition conflicts with the pattern of visual expectation, then confusion and rejection of the message may occur (Figure 2.1).

This perceptual phenomena has been intuitively understood and employed by painters of great works of art for centuries. Their work engages our attention and is visually satisfying. These masterpieces still communicate and satisfy because they are structured for visual understanding and their viewers respond intuitively to the underlying reinforcement of the visual system.

These perceptual characteristics can be converted into a set of building blocks that anyone can employ to achieve effective communication.

Definition of perception

This description of perception need not concern itself with a physical explanation of the mechanics of sight but with the process of perception as it affects camerawork and composition.

Figure 2.1 Perception is making sense of an image – searching for the best interpretation of the available data. The mind sees patterns and searches for the best interpretation. A perceived object is therefore a hypothesis to be tested against previous experience. If it looks like a duck then it is a duck. That is, until we see it as a rabbit.

The standard description of perception is that a physical object causes a change in the perceiver's sense-organ. This is known as 'stimulation' of the sense-organ. The stimulation causes an impulse to be first passed along a nerve to the brain. This in turn causes a change in the state of the brain. It is at the second stage of the process – 'a change in the state of the brain' that the straightforward nature of sight becomes problematic.

This change in the state of the brain causes a sensation in the mind of the perceiver. This sensation is then interpreted in the light of past experience as being a sensation of some specific sort – such as a sensation of blueness.
Philosophy in the Open Godfrey Vesey (ed.)

A sensation in the mind of the perceiver is not accessible to science and the individual deductions made cannot be monitored except by a description from the individual observer. Even so, in an attempt to understand this part of the perceptual process, a number of experiments have been carried out which rely on the observer reporting on their perceptual experience.

Characteristics of perception

There have been many theories about perception and many experiments – some of which appear to be contradictory. Most theorists agree that perception is instantaneous and not subject to extended judgement. It is an active exploration rather than a passive recording of the visual elements in the field of view and is selective and personal.

The mind makes sense of visual elements by grouping elements into patterns. Any stimulus pattern tends to be seen in such a way that the resulting structure is as simple as the given conditions permit. Making sense of visual stimuli involves testing by hypothesis. An unfamiliar or ambiguous image may be assigned a tentative definition until further information becomes available (Figure 2.2).

An American law lecturer once tested the accuracy of his students' ability to witness an event by staging a fake crime in his lecture hall. A man ran into the hall disrupting his lecture and brandished a

Figure 2.2 Searching for coherent shapes in a complex image, human perception will look for, and if necessary, create simple shapes. Straight lines will be continued by visual projection. (Cube shape from 'Organisational determinants of subjective contour.' Bradley)

weapon of some kind and then left. The law teacher immediately asked his students to accurately describe what they had seen. Needless to say every student 'witness' had a different version and a different description of the bogus criminal. The simple point was made that most people are selective in their viewpoint. They see what they expect to see or what they can understand.

What a person perceives is dependent on personal factors as well as the visual elements in their field of view. Their understanding of an image reflects past experiences as well as their present state of mind. Although it is probable that no two observers may observe a given scene in the same way and may disagree considerably as to its nature and contents, much of our perceptual experience shares common characteristics.

Whereas the camera is free of these subjective influences and simply records the image conditioned by mechanical properties of lens, camera position, exposure, etc., the cameraman can be affected by these influences unless he develops a visual eye. Hundreds of thousands of holiday snaps fail in their endeavour to record the experience of a holiday event because the holiday snappers failed to see what was in the viewfinder. They took a snap of what they imagined was there without checking to see what exactly was there.

Seeing an image as the camera sees it requires training the eye and brain. Understanding how we see is the first step in controlling visual communication.

How the mind responds to visual information

Much of the theory of perceptual characteristics has been influenced by Gestalt psychologists. Gestalt is the German word for 'form' and these psychologists held the view that it is the overall form of an image that we respond to not the isolated visual elements it contains. In general, we do not attempt to perceive accurately every detail of the shapes and objects perceived but select only as much as will enable us to identify what we see. This may depend on the

Figure 2.3 Organization by similar size. Although all the heads in the crowd are of similar size and create a pattern of visual unity, one face achieves prominence by its position in the frame and its familiarity.

probability of appearance of a particular type of object but the precision of our perception is sufficient only for our immediate need.

We may increase our visual concentration if we feel it is warranted but this enhanced visual attention may be of short duration. The tendency is for the perceptual system to group things into simple units.

The minimum amount of time needed to recognize an object (possibly 1/100 second) will depend on the familiarity and expectation of that specific image. An observer can perceive a large and complex vista that is seen everyday and anticipated, in a time which would be quite inadequate for the perception and understanding of a complex meaningless shape.

In searching for the best interpretation of the available visual data we utilize a number of perceptual 'shorthand' techniques which include the organization of similar shapes and similar sizes. Shapes that are similar are grouped and form a pattern that creates eye motion. A 'good' form, one which is striking and easy to perceive, is simple, regular, symmetrical and may have continuity in time. A 'bad' form without these qualities is modified by the perceiver to conform to 'good' form qualities (Figure 2.3).

Figure 2.4 (a)(b) Sometimes you cannot see the wood for the trees. A shift in camera position may establish figure/ground priorities and allow the subject to be emphasized.

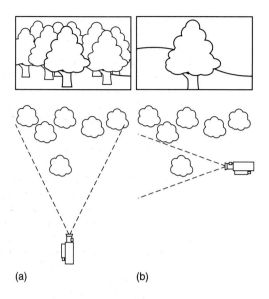

(a)   (b)

Perceptual steps

Perception is extraordinarily fast. This can be demonstrated by the deductions and judgements made when driving a car or as a pedestrian, the perceptual calculations made when crossing a busy city street. Each element of the perceptual steps may operate instantaneously or occur in an order conditioned by the visual situation.

First, there is the need to separate figure from ground. Figure describes the shape that is immediately observable whilst ground defines that shape by giving it a context. A chess piece is a figure with the chess board as its ground. Identifying the shape of the figure – that it is a pawn – may provide complete recognition. Other subject recognition may involve colour, brightness, texture, movement or spatial position. Instantaneous classification and identification occur continuously but the perceptual process can be helped or hindered by the presentation of the subject (Figures 2.4a and 2.4b).

If the image is familiar, recognition may be instantaneous and therefore there is a redundancy of information. If the image is unrecognized then there may be a rapid search and match through memory to find similarities in mental images. When an unexpected image cannot be identified then either a guess is made or it is ignored.

People habitually overlook things they cannot understand. For example, a foreign news story in a TV news bulletin in which the political context or geographic situation is unknown to the viewer, ceases to be information and is ignored unless a connection can be established with an existing frame of reference. The reporter, who may have lived with the story for days, weeks or even months, may have an abundance of background knowledge to the specific two-minute item he files that day. This may cause him to overestimate the background information the viewer brings to the story. A similar extended preparation and filming of a narrative sequence may involve the production group investigating and discussing every nuance and significance of a thirty-second shot. The first-time viewer of the shot has to extract all this day's/week's considered deliberations during the thirty-second running time of the shot.

We predict what is likely to happen next from our experience of the past and rely on these assumptions to forecast the future. Shot structure and shot composition have to take into account this habit of searching for the cause of an effect.

Problems with perception

There is a basic distinction between 'reading' the space in a two-dimensional image, where a hypothesis of shape, depth, etc. has to be estimated by viewing from a fixed position, compared to the potential, in a three-dimensional situation, to move within the space to confirm a hypothesis. We cannot walk around a picture.

Our perceptual knowledge is gained from our experience of moving in a three-dimensional world. An essential element of testing and checking perceptual information is by moving through space. We use these acquired three-dimensional perceptual skills and frequently apply them to a very reduced image depicted in two dimensions (e.g. a television screen) where we have no opportunity of testing out our depth 'guesses' by moving into the picture space.

Although the image created by a video or film camera may be similar to the image focused on the retina of the eye, there is the crucial difference of being unable to test out the depth indicators of a two-dimensional image by moving into its picture space. A moving camera can reproduce some of the image changes that occur when we move in space but not the visual depth checks achieved by binocular vision and head movement (Figures 2.5a–2.5c).

There is a considerable amount of visual information that is used in perception that is usually unacknowledged until an attempt is made to reproduce three dimensions on a two-dimensional plane. If an untrained person attempts to draw a townscape they will soon realize that there are many aspects of visual representation that they may never have been consciously aware of. Although information about perspective of line and mass and vanishing points are present in the eye they are un-examined even though they help us to determine distance.

We habitually underestimate the change in size of a person walking towards or away from us and mentally picture them modified in size but only with a slight alteration to their 'normal' size. An audience will appear from the front to have similar size

Figure 2.5 (a)(b)(c) A simple shape such as a cube is easily seen in isolation but is camouflaged when swallowed up in a more complex figure. The centre of interest of a composition requires visual emphasis. [Gollschadt diagram]

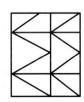

(a) (b) (c)

faces and yet the faces of the people in the back rows will probably be a tenth of the size of the faces of the people in the front row. We never recognize that the image of our face in the mirror is always much smaller than its actual size. These are all depth indicators we habitually ignore or make the necessary adjustment as in the phenomena of the 'upside down' image that is focused on the retina of the eye. We 'mentally' correct this inversion of our field of view.

The decrease in size of objects as they recede from us is used continuously to check on distance. In can also help to create a false distance. The final scene in 'Casablanca' is set inside an aircraft hanger with the doors open revealing an aeroplane. There was insufficient space in the studio to have an aircraft at the distance required so a scale model was built and 'casting' recruited midgets to sit at the lit windows. In 'Night of the Hunter' (1955) during the chase sequence in the swamp, a silhouette figure on a horseback crossing the skyline is not Robert Mitchum as implied in the story but a midget on a small pony.

As we move our viewpoint in space so the appearance of objects alters. A plate may have the shape of a circle seen from above but viewed from any other angle its shape is never circular but we persist with a mental image of a plate as a circle. We know that objects have an identity and a permanent form and ignore perceptual problems with the continuity of form which a changing viewpoint produces.

The two-dimensional representations of film and video provide image dimension or size relationship that we may not be aware of. Sometimes the appearance of everyday objects are altered when lit from an unfamiliar angle or seen in extreme close-up. A low angle, close shot of a golf ball against the sky in 'Murder by Contract' (1960) accompanied by the murmur of out-of-frame golfers established an expectation of the normal object size, until the camera pulled back and disclosed that the normal two-inch golf ball was in fact a four-foot high structure identifying the entrance to a golf course.

An unfamiliar setting or the absence of a field of reference for an object frequently creates difficulties in identifying what normally is recognized instantly. 'It looks like an "x" but I must look at it longer to make quite sure' can be caused by unexpected lighting or shot size. The meaning of a familiar image can be understood without conscious thought whereas intelligent interest is required to understand unfamiliar subjects. Recognition of images may be easily accomplished if the observer is favourably disposed towards them. That which tends to arouse the observer's hostility or antipathy may be either forgotten or ignored.

A tight shot of a woman's face looking down to a baby at her breast will engender in most people a feeling of warmth and human empathy. It is universal and timeless and will in general produce a feeling of uncritical endorsement. The same activity if framed in a wider shot now showing mother and child in an exterior that includes shabby and broken coaches and caravans, dirty and half-clothed children and a few mangy dogs roaming around a wood fire will set up a completely different set of responses. Putting the original subject in a social context will provoke the viewer into bringing preconceived attitudes and social judgements to bear on the activity. It may even provoke anger that a woman should bring a child into

Figure 2.6 Visual illusion, the
Penrose triangle. Even though we
are aware that an image is an
illusion (an impossible construction
in reality) we are still persuaded by
perceptual clues that its structure is
plausible. The normal perceptual
conclusions override our intellectual
understanding of the illusion.

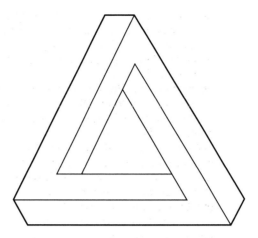

the world in such an inhospitable and alien (to the viewer's frame of
reference) world. What is *included* and *excluded* from the frame
alters the way the central subject is understood (Figure 2.6).

Attention and perception

Perception is dependent on attention. If attention is concentrated on
a small part of the field of view, little will be perceived of the rest
of the scene. If attention is spread over a large area, no one part will
be very clearly and accurately perceived. The total amount which can
be attended to at any one moment is constant.

There is normally selective perception in everyday life with people
unable to attend to two different visual events and they either
combine the two or their attention ends. It is not possible to continually attend to even one part of an image. After a short period,
attention wanders but by directing perception understanding
improves (Figure 2.7).

Attention can be split three ways even when watching a familiar
TV event such as a weather forecast. The physical appearance of the
forecaster as well as their spoken commentary will split the attention and to this is added a third part of the image that requires attention – the changing graphics of the weather chart. It is difficult to
attend to all three elements even in this simple display without loss
of attention to one part of the information presented.

Figure 2.7 Our attention is almost
immediately captured by the 'one'
that is different. The repetition of
the brick shape provides an overall
image unity whilst at the same
time emphasizing the one
exception.

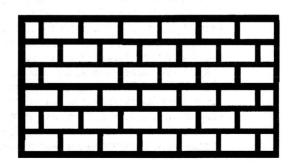

Summary

The mind tends to group objects together into one single comprehensive image. The mind sees patterns and composition can enhance or facilitate this tendency or it can prevent it. A knowledge of how the mind groups visual elements is therefore a valuable tool for good communication. Test the strength of a composition by examining the individual visual elements it contains and check if they separately or collectively strengthen or weaken the overall form.

3
Perspective

Art and photography

A nineteenth-century view about the history of art was that painters
had struggled for many centuries in the quest for a convincing representation of the world but were finally beaten to the post by the
invention of photography. The photographic image was thought to
bring a new standard of objectivity in depicting a three-dimensional
object in two dimensions. The fallacy of considering the photographic image as an impartial depiction of an event is matched by
the assumption that painting is solely concerned with a convincing
representation of a specific field of view.

Any camera – still, film or video – cannot record an image without
leaving an imprint of the optical properties of its lens, its position in
space and some indication of the reasons for selecting that lens
position.

There is a widespread assumption that whereas a painter's preoc-
cupations may influence his vision, the TV or film camera is a fairly
straightforward device for converting a subject into a two-dimensional image.

The camera is never free from distortion. There are a number of
conditioning elements that convert the original image into a two-
dimensional image including loss of binocular vision, a selective
frame which excludes as well includes, a change in perspective and
so on.

Secondly, even if these distortions could be kept to a minimum,
there is still the problem that the image is a selected message which
has to be decoded by the viewer. The camera stands between the
viewer and the original subject and apart from the preconceived
attitudes the viewer brings to the images presented to him, the
cameraman also brings his assumptions and professional values (invisible techniques) to bear on the message. In E. H. Gombrich's words

However faithful an image that serves to convey visual information may be,
the process of selection will always reveal the maker's interpretation of what
he considers relevant.

'The Image and the Eye'

It is a highly subjective activity and both the methods of perception (viewer and cameraman) and the 'professional' values that the cameraman brings to the subject will affect what is communicated. One of the crucial factors that conditions the 'look' of the shot concerns perspective.

The structural skeleton of a shot

Although a television or film image is viewed as a two-dimensional picture, most shots will contain depth indicators that allows the audience to understand the two-dimensional representation of space that contains the action. Text on a blank background has no depth indicators but the text is still perceptually seen as 'in front' of the page.

The audience will be looking at the surface of the screen, a two-dimensional plane covered by a series of lines, shapes, brightness points, contrasts, colour, etc., and will respond to any indication of recognizable form and space contained in the shot. They will read into the two-dimensional image an impression of a three-dimensional space.

There are therefore two aspects of the composition. The content – a house, horse or face – and the front surface (see Chapter 5 for definition) arrangements of lines, shapes, contrasts, etc. which form the recognizable images. The majority of the audience may only remember the content of the shot – the house, horse or face – but they will also be affected by the series of lines, shapes, brightness points and contrasts, colour, etc. which constructs the front surface plane of the image. This 'abstract' element of the shot may be crucial to the way the viewer responds to the image.

Each visual element in a shot can therefore serve two functions:

1 As *content* – that part of the composition that provides depth indicators and information about the physical subject of the shot.
2 As *form* – part of the design that lies on the surface plane of the screen and forms an overall abstract design which can produce a reaction in the viewer independent of any response to the content of the shot.

The reduction of this aspect of the shot, its form, to a simplified diagram of line and shape has been termed the structural skeleton of the image. It reveals the perceptual elements that potentially can hold the viewer's attention over and above the interest in the content of the shot.

The construction of the structural skeleton of the plane of the shot does not simply rely on content. For example, every cameraman knows that a shot of a building, can be made more interesting if the camera is moved from a square-on symmetrical viewpoint to an angle of view favouring more than one side or surface and/or if the height of the lens is varied. Re-positioning the camera is altering the structural skeleton for, while the content of the shot remains and is recognizable as 'a building', converging lines of rooftop, windows, doors, etc. have been altered and restructured to provide a more pleasing 'front surface' design (Figures 3.1a and 3.1b).

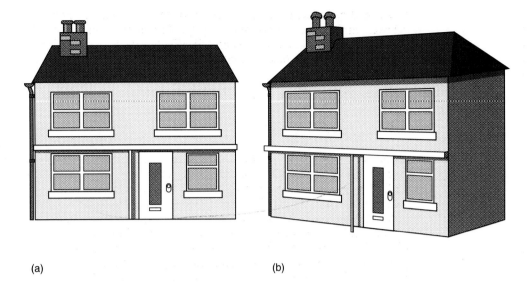

(a)   (b)

Figure 3.1 (a)(b) Diagonal
arrangements of lines in a
composition produce a greater
impression of vitality than either
vertical or horizontal lines. The
square-on shot of a house is
visually static because it maximizes
the number of horizontal lines in
the frame. Angling the camera
position to show two sides of a
building converts the horizontal
lines into diagonals. A line at an
angle is perceptually seen as a line
that is in motion. Compositions
with a strong diagonal element
imply movement or vitality (see
Chapter 5, Line).
 Although the subject of the shot
remains the same – a house – the
structural skeleton of the shot has
been rearranged to increase the
viewer's perceptual attention
independent of their interest in the
specific content of the shot.

The degree to which these convergencies can be controlled by lens
height, lens position and lens-angle requires an understanding of
perspective. One of the pre-occupations of fifteenth-century painting was an investigation of perspective. An understanding of their
visual rediscoveries helps the cameraman to appreciate the effect of
lens and camera position on film and TV composition.

Depth indicators and their relationship to the lens

The mathematical laws by which objects appear to diminish in size
as they recede from us, the way parallel lines appear to converge and
vanish at the horizon, were introduced to western art in the fifteenth
century.

'The Profanation of the Host', (Figure 3.2), is a detail of a painting by the Florentine artist Paolo Uccello. As you can see, he has
used all the newly discovered linear perspective indicators to represent depth on a two-dimensional surface. They include converging
parallel lines such as the timbers in the ceiling, the tiles on the floor
and the walls, and a reduction in the size of the tiles as they recede.

So what are the laws of perspective that need to be understood?
Unlike the Renaissance artist, the cameraman does not have to
puzzle over how to represent a two-dimensional plan of a three-
dimensional view before he produces a realistic picture. He does not
have to analyse how the eye perceives depth. He simply presses the
record button and the camera does the rest. Or does it?

The cameraman has to decide at what distance and with what lens-
angle he will shoot the scene. That will make a difference to the size
relationships within the frame – he will control the perspective of
mass.

He has to decide the lens height. Shooting low with a level camera
will produce one type of line perspective. Shooting from a high

Figure 3.2 A detail from 'The Profanation of the Host' (1465), a painting by the Florentine artist Paolo Uccello where he explores the newly discovered linear perspective indicators to represent depth on a two-dimensional surface.

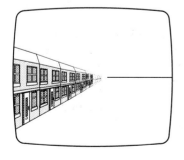

Figure 3.3 All parallel horizontal lines that recede into the distance appear to converge towards the horizon at one point known as the vanishing point. If the camera is level (i.e. without tilt), the horizon line will bisect the frame at mid-point. A line projected from the camera to the vanishing point will intersect all objects at a height equivalent to the lens.

vantage point tilted down will produce another set of line relationships in the frame.

The camera doesn't lie – much. It simply reproduces an image conditioned by one of the four parameters mentioned above – lens-height, camera tilt, distance from subject and lens-angle.

When a camera converts a three-dimensional scene into a television or film picture, it leaves an imprint of these four decisions. We can detect these decisions in any image by examining:

1 the position of the horizon line and where it cuts similar sized figures – this will reveal camera height and tilt;
2 any parallel converging lines in the image such as the edges of buildings or roads – this will also reveal lens-height and camera-tilt;
3 the size relationship between foreground and background objects particularly the human figure – this will gives clues to camera distance from objects and lens-angle;
4 camera distance from subject will be revealed by the change in object size when moving towards or away from the lens.

For any specific lens-angle and camera position there will be a unique set of the above parameters. The internal 'perspective' of the picture is created by the focal length of the lens except, of course, where false perspective has been deliberately created.

Vanishing point

All parallel horizontal lines that recede into the distance appear to converge towards the horizon line. Receding parallel lines above

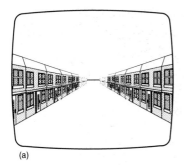

(a)

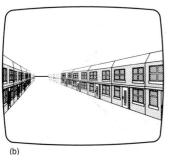

(b)

(c)

Figure 3.4 (a) A single vanishing point in the centre of the frame (e.g. level camera positioned in the centre of a street looking along the street) will produce a very centralized composition with all the parallel lines of the houses meeting in the centre of the frame. **(b)** Panning the camera right will push the vanishing point to the left of the frame and produce a different set of converging lines. **(c)** A common compositional device to emphasize the principal subject in the frame is to place the vanishing point just outside the frame so that the strongly converging lines draw the eye to the main subject.

eye-line slope down, receding lines below eye-level appear to slope up towards the horizon (Figure 3.3). The position of the vanishing point in the frame will control the degree of convergence of any parallel lines to the line of the lens-axis.

A single vanishing point in the centre of the frame (e.g. level camera positioned in the centre of a street looking along the street with lens at half-house height) will produce a very centralized composition with all the parallel lines of the houses meeting in the centre of frame. It could emphasize, for example, the conformity and rigidity in the planning of a housing estate but the shot may have little or no compositional elements that hold the attention (Figure 3.4a).

Panning the camera right will push the vanishing point to the left of the frame and produce a different set of converging lines (Figure 3.4b). Continuing to pan the camera right will position the vanishing point outside the frame (Figure 3.4c) and progressively reduce the angle of convergence of parallel lines until they become horizontal at the point when the lens axis is at 90° to them.

A very popular compositional device to emphasize the principal subject in the frame by focusing the strongly convergent lines behind the subject is to place the vanishing point just outside the frame.

Tilting the camera

Panning the camera up will move the horizon line down and redistribute the proportion of the converging lines so that the upper set of lines will have a steeper angle than the lower lines. Panning the camera down will move the horizon line up and will have the reverse effect.

A third influence on the degree of convergence will be camera position. Moving the camera back and using a longer focal length lens to keep in frame the original houses will reduce the angle of convergence. Moving the camera forward and using a shorter focal length lens will increase the angle of convergence (Figures 3.5a and 3.5b).

The final influence on the structural skeleton of lines will be to increase or decrease the camera height. Craning up and panning down will produce one set of converging lines. Craning down and panning up will create another set of lines.

These four camera parameters – camera height, tilt, lens-angle and camera position – in combination or singularly, all influence the structural skeleton of the shot without altering content.

Two-point vanishing perspective

A camera positioned at the corner of a building with a lens positioned at half-building height will produce a shot with two vanishing points. Depending on the framing and content, the vanishing points may be inside or outside the frame.

Again the four camera parameters listed above will have a significant effect on the convergence of lines. Using a very wide angle lens combined with a camera position close to the building will create the greatest angles of convergence.

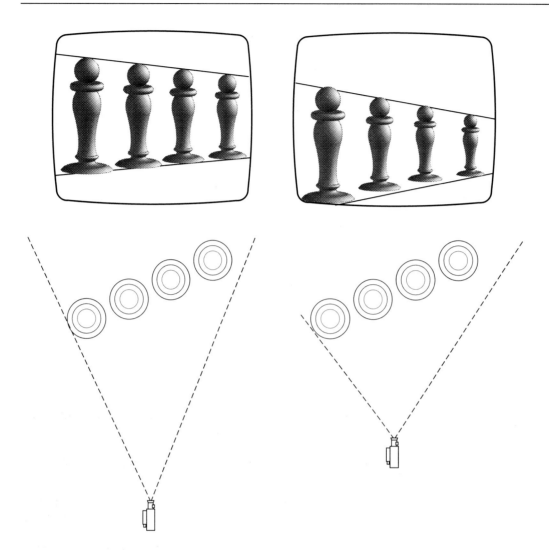

Figure 3.5 A significant influence on the degree of linear convergence is the distance of the camera from the main subject. Moving the camera back (a) and using a longer focal length lens to keep in frame the foreground chess pieces will reduce the angle of convergence of a projected line at the top and at the base of the other chess pieces. Moving the camera forward (b) and using a shorter focal length lens will increase the angle of convergence.

Three-point linear perspective

If a camera is looking at the corner of a very tall building at lens position of eye height and is panned up to include the whole building a third set of converging vertical lines is added to the two sets of horizontal converging lines. There are now three vanishing points in the frame with the additional flexibility of altering all the angles of convergencies with camera height, lens-angle, camera distance from building and angle of tilt (Figure 3.6).

Multiple vanishing points

Any number of vanishing points are created depending on the variety and position of parallel horizontal and vertical lines in relationship to the camera lens. For example, a high camera angle looking down on the rooftops of a village has little control over the structural skeleton of the shot apart from adjustment in framing. This becomes unimportant because the variety and interaction of the

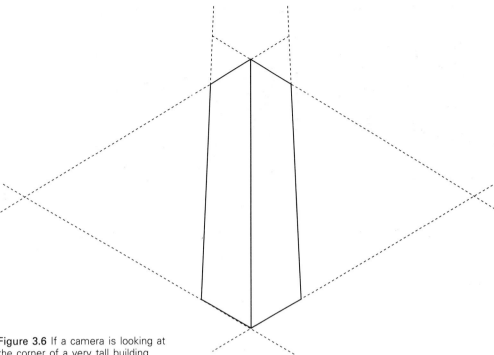

Figure 3.6 If a camera is looking at the corner of a very tall building and is panned up to include the whole building, a third set of converging vertical lines is added to the two sets of horizontal converging lines.

lines usually gives the shot sufficient visual interest without the need to control the angle of convergence.

Horizon line and camera height as a compositional device

Our normal perceptual experience of someone of our own size moving on flat ground towards us is that the horizon line will always intersect behind them at eye level.

It was a fifteenth-century writer/architect, Leon Alberti, who realized that the controlling factor when creating a three-dimensional effect on a two-dimensional plane was the distance of the 'recording' eye from the scene and its height from the ground.

The crucial element in his construct was the horizon line. This illusionary line where the ground plane meets the sky is also the point where all orthogonals, that is, parallel lines running at right angles to the horizon line, meet. This point is called the vanishing point.

We are usually most aware of the horizon line when we are by the sea. If we set up a horizontally level camera at eye level beside the sea it follows from Alberti's reasoning that as only horizontal lines can ever reach the horizon, the horizon line will appear to be at the mid-point vertically in the frame. It will bisect the frame at its mid-point because only the centre axis of the vertical lens-angle is horizontal (Figures 3.7a–3.7c).

If the camera is level, the centre axis of the lens will always be the only horizontal line that meets the horizon therefore increasing or decreasing the lens height has no effect on the position of the horizon line in frame.

Figure 3.7
(a)(b)(c) If the camera is level (i.e. without any degree of tilt), the horizon line will always bisect the centre of the shot independent of the height of the camera. It will cross the frame at mid-point because the centre axis of the lens-angle is the only horizontal line that meets the horizon. Increasing or decreasing a level camera has no effect on the position of the horizon line in the frame.

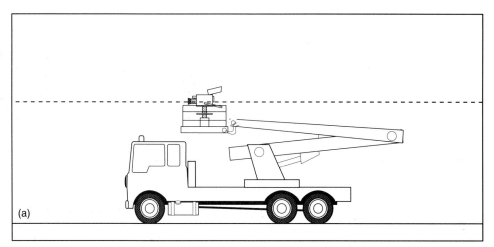

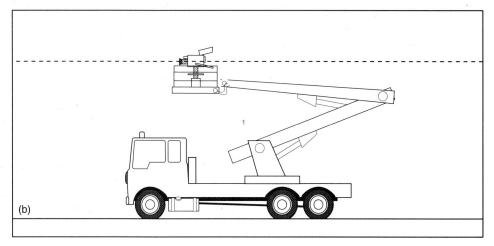

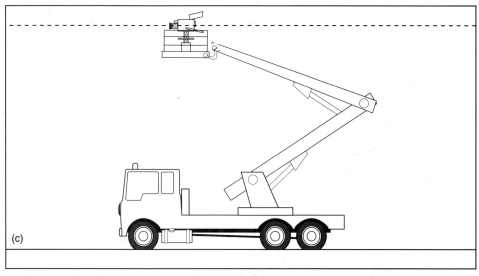

(a)   (b)   (c)

Figure 3.8 On a flat surface, the horizon line cuts similar size figures at the same point. The height of that point is the height of the lens. The position of the horizon line is controlled by the degree of camera tilt. (a) Low angle; (b) lens at eye height; (c) high angle

Of course Alberti's explanation of our normal perception of linear perspective does involve two visual illusions. The first illusion is that the sky meets the sea when it obviously does not; secondly, that a visual sight line parallel to the sea would eventually meet this illusionary line at what is termed the vanishing point.

Looking from behind the camera, we will see that the horizon line will intersect the camera at lens height. If the lens height is 1.5 metres then all 1.5 metre objects in front of the lens will be cut at the same point by the horizon line in the frame.

If we tilt the camera down, the horizon line moves up the frame. If we tilt up, the line moves down. But if we crane the camera up, keeping it level, the horizon line follows and continues to bisect the frame.

If the camera is level, any object between the lens and the illusionary vanishing point on the horizon will be intersected by the horizon line at the same height as the lens (Figures 3.8a–3.8c).

American silent film production at the turn of the twentieth century used a convention of a 50 mm lens at eye level and actor movement was restricted to being no closer to the lens than 12 ft. With an actor standing 12 ft from the lens, the bottom of the frame cuts him at knee height. By 1910, the Vitagraph company allowed the actors to play up to 9 ft from the lens and the camera was lowered to chest height (see Chapter 8, Lens-angle and camera position).

From these static camera positions there developed a Hollywood convention of frequently placing the camera at eye level which in turn allowed the horizon line to cut the foreground actors at eye level. It is particularly noticeable in exteriors in Westerns made before the 1960s. Whether the artistes are standing or sitting, the camera is often positioned at eye height which places the horizon behind the eyes. This emphasizes the main subject of the frame – the face – and the main area of interest of the face – the eyes (Figure 3.9).

A more prosaic factor controlling lens height is the need to avoid shooting off the top of studio sets. Keeping the camera at eye level speeds up production as actor movement to camera can be accommodated without panning up and shooting off the top of the set or the need to relight.

Lens height will also control the way the audience identifies with the subject. Orson Welles, in the film 'Touch of Evil' (1958), played a fat corrupt detective in a Mexican border town. He directed the

Figure 3.9 If the camera is at eye level, the horizon line (if it is in frame) will pass behind the foreground actors at eye level. This emphasizes the main subject of the frame – the face, and the main area of interest of the face – the eyes.

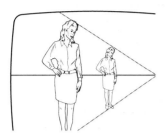

Figure 3.10 Size relationships are proportional to the distance of the subjects from the camera. The image of a 1.5 metre subject 2 metres from the lens will be twice as large as the image of a 1.5 metre subject 4 metres from the camera whatever lens-angle is used.

film and by using a wide-angle lens and placing the camera at a low height looking up at this character, he created a brooding dominant personality who appeared to be towering over the audience and almost falling forwards on to them. The impression produced by this lens height and angle was of an unstable but powerful figure.

Moving the horizon down below a person makes them more dominant because the viewer is forced to adopt a lower eyeline viewpoint. We are in the size relationship of children looking up to adults. Leni Riefenstahl's film 'Triumph of the Will' (1934) about the 1934 Nazi Party Nuremberg Rally has frequent low angle shots of Adolf Hitler. It increases his height and status and is contrasted with the high-angle 'bird's eye views' of the massed ranks of his followers.

A low lens height may also de-emphasize floor or ground level detail because we are looking along at ground level and reducing or eliminating indications of ground space between objects. This concentrates the viewer's interest on the vertical subjects.

A high position lens height has the reverse effect. The many planes of the scene are emphasized like a scale model. The viewer is in a 'God-like' privileged position observing more than the participants in the scene. We are now adults looking down on children.

Usually it is better to divide the frame into unequal parts by positioning the horizon line above or below the mid-point of the frame. Many cameramen intuitively use the Rule of Thirds (see Chapter 8) to position the horizon. A composition can evoke space by panning up and placing the line low in frame. Placing a high horizon in the frame can balance a darker foreground land mass or subject with the more attention grabbing detail of a high key sky. It also helps with contrast range and exposure.

Camera distance

Our normal perceptual experience of someone of our own size moving on flat ground towards us is that the horizon line will always intersect behind them at eye level. Looking at the 'Profanation of the Host' painting (Figure 3.2) one can observe that Uccello has reduced the size of the tiles as they recede from the observer. The ratio of size change puzzled many painters until Alberti showed the common-sense arithmetic of how the reduction in size is directly proportional to the distance from the eye.

A 1.5 metre woman 2 metres from the lens will produce an image that is twice as large as a 1.5 metre woman 4 metres from the camera (Figure 3.10).

Size relationships or the perspective of mass can be confused with the wide angle effect and the narrow angle effect. By this I mean that to increase the size of a background figure to a foreground figure it is common practice to reposition the camera back and zoom in to return to the original framing. The size relationships have now altered. It is not the narrower angle that produced this effect but the increased distance from the camera (Figures 3.11a–3.11c).

By tracking away from the two figures we have altered the ratio between lens and first figure and lens and second figure. It is a much smaller ratio and therefore the difference in size between the two of them is now not so great. When we zoom in and revert to the original full frame for foreground figure we keep the new size relationships

(a)

(b)

(c)

Figure 3.11 The distance between the two figures remains unchanged in all three illustrations. The distance between foreground figure and camera has altered. With each camera reposition, lens-angle of zoom is adjusted to keep the foreground figure the same size in the frame. The 'wide angle' effect and the 'narrow angle effect' is a product of the camera distance from subjects. (a) Mid-range; (b) wide angle; (c) narrow angle.

that have been formed by camera distance. The two figures appear to be closer in size.

As part of our perception of depth depends on judging size relationships – the further away the smaller they are – our perception of this new size relationship produced by tracking out and zooming in leads us to believe that the distance between equal height figures is not so great as the first framing.

Possibly, the narrow angle and the wide angle effect is mis-named. It should be called the distant viewing effect. Our eyes cannot zoom and therefore we are not so conscious of size relationships changing in normal perception.

The important point to remember is that subject size relationship is a product of camera distance. How the subject fills the frame is a product of lens-angle. This, of course, is the crucial distinction between tracking and zooming. Tracking the camera towards or away from the subject alters size relationships – the perspective of mass. Zooming the lens, preserves the existing size relationships and magnifies or diminishes a portion of the shot (see Chapter 10, 'Camera Movement').

Lens-angle

The choice of lens-angle and camera distance from the subject is the controlling factor in the way that depth is depicted in the image. This subject is treated in more detail in 'Staging' but the 'internal' space of a shot often plays a crucial part in setting up the atmosphere of a shot.

Figure 3.12 (a) 'The Last Supper', Leonardo da Vinci.

A long lens positioned at a distance from a cramped interior will heighten the claustrophobia of the setting. Subject size ratios will be evened out from foreground to background and movement to and away from camera will show no significant change in size and therefore give a subjective impression that no distance has been traversed.

Both compression of space and the reduction of apparent movement caused problems in the editing of an 'all action' film where a shot of two people struggling on a railway line with a train in the distance was shot with a long lens. The visual impression, due to the compression of space, was that the train was nearly upon them whereas the narrative required a great deal more action before that point was reached. Secondly, because the train appeared to have little change in size over the duration of the shot, it had the appearance of moving slowly. This negated its threat to the protagonists and reduced the build-up of tension. A wide-angle lens close to the subject will increase space, emphasize movement and depending on shot content, emphasize convergence of line and contrast of mass.

Placement of vanishing points

Control of convergence becomes important when it is used to focus attention on the main subject of the shot. Converging lines can be used to bring this foreground subject into prominence (see Figure 3.4c). The positioning of the vanishing point controls the convergence angles of receding parallel lines. By titling or panning the camera the vanishing points can be placed within or outside the frame. Where the vanishing point is positioned will have a considerable influence on the composition.

Look at Figure 3.12a, Leonardo da Vinci's 'The Last Supper' (page 27). Check to see where Leonardo has placed the vanishing point of the ceiling beams and side panels.

Figure 3.12b shows that Leonardo chose a central vanishing point (where all orthogonals – receding parallels perpendicular to the picture plane) converge on the head of Christ. This 'implosion' of converging lines is in contrast to the square on table position which in general tends to reduce the dynamic impact of an image. Placing

Figure 3.12 (b) The 'implosion' of the projected converging lines of the ceiling and side panels meeting behind the head of Christ emphasize his central importance in the composition.

Figure 3.13 The screen size of the reproduced image will increase proportionally to the viewing distance if the original perspective experienced by the observer at distance 'z' from the subject is to be duplicated.

The viewing distance 'z' of screen A is too close to reproduce a 'natural' perspective and would simulate a 'wide angle' look at that viewing distance.

Screen B would simulate a 'narrow angle' view point because the screen size is too small for viewing distance 'z'.

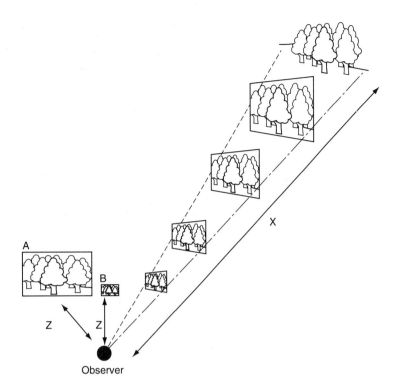

the vanishing point at the central subject emphasizes the subject as being the centre of the view and therefore psychologically in this viewpoint, the centre of the world. If the vanishing point of these strong converging lines was placed outside the frame or at the edge of the frame, the main subject of the painting could be seen as just another element in the frame.

Many cameramen, in framing up a shot, will look to maximize the convergence of lines by choice of lens-angle and camera height/position. Shooting square-on to a subject usually keeps the vanishing point within the frame and often results in a strong emphasis on symmetry and simple balance particularly if there are strong horizontal lines in the frame at 90° to the lens axis. By shooting at an oblique angle, the vanishing point is moved out of the frame and there is a greater emphasis of converging orthogonals. These form dominant groups of receding wedge shapes and give a greater dynamic attack to the image compared to strong level horizontal lines. Visual excitement is created by neighbouring parallel lines getting closer and closer together.

'Normal' perspective

If an observer looks at a field of view through an empty picture frame held at arms length, he will require the frame to be progressively increased in size the greater the distance the frame is positioned away from him in order that the same field-of-view is contained within the frame at all times (Figure 3.13).

As we have discussed, the perspective of mass and the perspective of line are created by the distance of the subjects from the observer.

Size relationships and convergence of line in his field of view will depend on their distance from him. Therefore if he does not change his position, the perspective appearance of the 'image' within the frame will remain unchanged. The frame will simply get larger and larger the further it is from the observer's position.

If a photograph was substituted for the frame and increasingly enlarged to match frame size, the two factors which control the exact replication of perspective characteristics in an image are revealed as image size and the distance of the image from the observer.

No lens produces a 'wrong' perspective provided the viewer views the correct size image at the taking distance. A wide-angle shot taken close to the principal subject would require the viewer almost to press their nose to the screen in order to experience the perspective characteristics of the image that they would experience if they had been the camera.

The calculation of which lens-angle provides 'correct' perspective (i.e. equivalent to an observer replacing the camera) must include image size of reproduction and the distance the viewer is to the screen. A person sitting in the back row of a cinema may be viewing a screen size that is a tenth of the size the audience in the front is experiencing. There is no lens-angle that can provide both viewing distances with 'correct' perspective. Audience in the front row will experience wide-angle shots as having 'correct' perspective whilst the audience in the back row may judge narrower angle shots as having more 'correct' perspective.

Often the requirements of a script require interpretation rather than precise replication of 'correct' perspective. Interpretative compositions can therefore be created using perspective characteristics which expand or flatten space.

To visually represent the sensation of vertigo, Alfred Hitchcock, in a famous shot in 'Vertigo' (1958), had the camera tracking in matched to a zoom-out to keep the visual elements at the edge of the frame static (see Figure 10.3). Because the camera was moving closer to the subject, the image size relationships and line convergence in the frame changed and gave a greater impression of depth to the shot. The zoom-out compensated by keeping the same size image of the foreground subject producing an effect of space expanding without movement.

Estimating distance

There are a number of perceptual clues that are used to estimate distance or space. The depth indicators include binocular vision which allows convergent and divergent movement to be estimated by the use of 'two' viewpoints. Subjects moving towards or away from the observer alter the size of the image focused on the retina of the eye. This change in size may not be accurately appreciated as perception often involves deductions from what is known rather than what is seen. Objects that overlap and their size relationship, if they are similar sized objects, indicate their relative position in space. Colour change due to atmospheric haze and hazy outline at long distance also aid depth perception. Similar objects moving at different velocities also indicate their spatial relationship.

All these depth indicators can be used in film and television composition not only to replicate normal perceptual experiences but also to create atmosphere or to interpret narrative requirements.

Summary

Any camera – still, film or video – cannot record an image without leaving an imprint of the optical properties of its lens, its position in space and some indication of the reasons for selecting that lens position. One of the crucial factors that conditions the 'look' of the shot concerns perspective.

The form ('structural skeleton') of a shot, its dominant lines and shapes, can potentially hold the viewer's attention over and above the interest in the content of the shot. The construction of this 'structural skeleton' is dependent on the distance of the camera from the subject and the lens-angle, which control the size relationships within the frame – the perspective of mass.

The choice of lens-angle and camera distance from the subject is the controlling factor in the way that depth is depicted in the image. Lens height and camera tilt will control line perspective. Shooting low with a level camera will produce one type of line perspective. Shooting from a high vantage point tilted down will produce another set of line relationships in the frame.

The important point to remember is that subject size relationship is a product of camera distance. How the subject fills the frame is a product of lens-angle. This is the crucial distinction between tracking and zooming.

4
Frame and aspect ratio

Frame – an invisible focus of power

At the same moment that we perceive the identity of an object within a frame, we are also aware of the spatial relationship between the object and the frame. Perceptual psychologists have established that observers will unconsciously imply potential motion to a static object depending on its position within the frame. A single object will either be 'pulling' towards the centre or to the corners and/or edge of the frame. A field of forces can be plotted (Figure 4.1), which plots the position of rest or balance (centre and mid-point on the diagonal between corner and centre) and positions of ambiguity where the observer cannot predict the potential motion of the object and therefore an element of perceptual unease is created. Whether the object is passively attracted by centre or edge or whether the object actively moved of its own volition depends on content.

The awareness of motion of a static visual element with relation to the frame is an intrinsic part of perception. It is not an intellectual judgement tacked on to the content of an image based on previous experience, but an integral part of perception. The edge of the frame and also the shape of the frame therefore have a strong influence on composition.

Figure 4.1 A single object will either be 'pulling' towards the centre or to the corners and/or edge of the frame. There are also positions of ambiguity where an observer cannot predict the potential motion of the object.

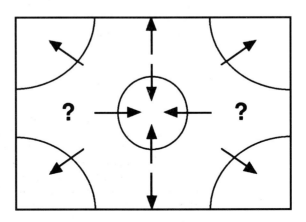

(a)

(b)

(c)

Figure 4.2 There is a strong perceptual awareness of the invisible reference points of the frame. (a) If the camera is panned up, a point is reached, with a large amount of headroom, where the subject appears to be slipping out of the bottom of the frame. (b) Panning down to create a shot with no headroom produces the feeling that the subject is leaving through the top of the frame. (c) There is a point of equilibrium where the subject is balanced against the invisible forces of the frame.

The pattern of a photographic image is more than the relationship between size, shape, brightness differences and colour contrast of the visual elements, there is also a hidden structural pattern created by the frame. An image contains more than the visible elements that make up the shot and these 'unseen' aspects can exert a powerful influence on the composition. As we saw in the discussion on perspective, an observer can be aware of the position of the vanishing point (within or outside of the frame) even if it is not self-evidently indicated.

These frame 'field' of forces exert pressure on the objects contained within the frame and any adjustment to the composition of a group of visual elements will be arranged with reference to these pressures. This strong perceptual awareness of the invisible reference points of the frame can be demonstrated by examining a simple medium close-up shot framed with normal headroom. If the camera is panned up, a point is reached, with a large amount of headroom, where the subject appears to be slipping out of the bottom of the frame. Panning down to create a shot with no headroom produces the feeling that the subject is leaving through the top of the frame (Figures 4.2a–4.2c).

Framing anything towards the corners gives the impression that the subject matter is slipping away from the dead centre reference point. Placing the subject dead centre of the frame resists or balances out the 'pulling effect' of the corners. By eliminating tension an image results that lacks visual excitement because there is no visual stress within the frame. The subject is at such a condition of equilibrium that it lacks any visual energy (Figure 4.3a–4.3c).

A different placement of the subject within the frame's 'field of forces' can therefore induce a perceptual feeling of equilibrium, of motion or of ambiguity.

Viewfinder as an editing tool

The viewfinder is selective – it excludes as well includes visual material. The frame of a shot creates an 'enclosure', a fence that separates the image from its environment – a bright rectangle surrounded by blackness. To some extent (ignoring size) a film image is viewed in a darkened cinema in a similar condition as an optical viewfinder on a camera. A video viewfinder image, however, is seen by the cameraman in very different conditions to the television

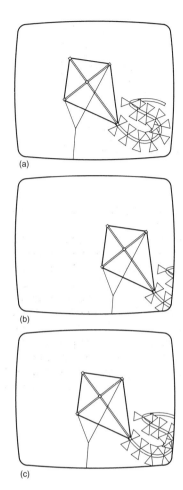

Figure 4.3 (a) When the main subject is centre frame there is little or any tension set up between frame and subject. (b) Offsetting the subject to this degree suggests that the frame is ahead of the kite. There is a marked contrast between the space in the left of the frame and the kite. It is ambiguous visual communication as it could imply that either the kite is losing height or that it has unlimited space to climb. (c) Placing the subject too close to centre can also be ambiguous as it remains unclear whether the kite is moving to equilibrium or is being pulled towards one of the sides of the frame.

viewer. But both optical and electronic viewfinders display images that deviate in significant ways to our normal experience of perception.

Static viewpoint

Human perception is unable to be as static and as continuously focused and attentive on a selected portion of a field of view as a camera. Attention, after a short period of time, will inevitably be captured by movement or noise from visual subjects outside the selected zone of view. The camera can continue its static unblinking gaze until altered by the cameraman.

A hard cut-off

There is no awareness of what lies outside the selected viewfinder image except by deduction based on content or previous shots. By selective editing, a completely fictitious environment can be suggested to lie outside the hard cut-off point of the frame. Human perception has the ability to focus on one section of its view whilst being aware of visual activity on the edge of the field of view.

One of the early Hollywood conventions was to compose the shot so that it contained the action within the frame and then by cutting, followed the action in discrete, complete shots. Each shot was self-contained and referred only to what is seen and shuts out or excludes anything outside of the frame. This is the *closed frame* technique and is structured in such a way as to keep the attention only on the information that is contained in the shot. If there is any significant reference to a subject outside of the frame, then there is a cut or a camera move to bring the referred subject into frame. This convention is still followed in many different types of programme format. For example, in a television cooking demonstration, the demonstrator in medium close-up (MCU) may refer to some ingredient they are about to use which is outside the frame. Either the MCU is immediately loosened to reveal the ingredient or there is a cutaway to a close-up of them.

The *open frame* convention allows action to move in and out of the frame. An example would be a character in a hallway who would be held on screen whilst in dialogue with someone who is moving in, and out of, frame whilst entering and leaving various rooms which are unseen. Their movement while they are out of frame is implied and not cut to as separate shots. The *open frame* does not disguise the fact that the shot is only a partial viewpoint of a much larger environment. This technique considers that it is not necessary for the audience to see the reality beyond the shot in order to be convinced that it exists (Figures 4.4a and 4.4b).

In the mid-nineteenth century, the increased speed of film emulsion allowed faster exposure and the ability to capture movement. Photographs of street scenes now became possible and often featured, by chance, people on the edge of frame either moving into or out of the shot. These snapshot 'chance' compositions appealed to painters such as Degas (see Figure 8.3) who used the same convention of objects on the edge of frame to add to the dynamics of the composition (see Chapter 5, Dissonance) and as a

Figure 4.4 (a) A **closed frame** contains all the relevant action. (b) An **open frame** requires the audience to assume what they cannot see – that there is a door and keyhole beyond the confines of the frame.

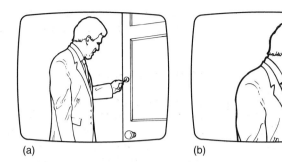

(a)   (b)

pointer to the arbitrary nature of the placing of the frame which excluded a greater reality outside the frame.

Some film directors, such as Antonioni, have emphasized the arbitrary nature of the frame as a device which switches on pieces of 'reality' only when required, by holding the shot of a location when any significant action has ended. For example, the shot may continue of an empty room when the actors have exited to under-line the continuing existence of the room independent of staged action or the demands of the narrative. This is similar to the attitude expressed in the two humorous limericks Ronald Knox penned as a refutation of the philosophy of George Berkeley who maintained that material objects only exist through being perceived. A tree, for example, would cease to exist if no one was looking at it (or as soon as it was cutaway from!).

There was a young man who said, 'God
Must think it exceedingly odd
If he finds that this tree
Continues to be
When there's no one about in the Quad'.

With the reply:

Dear Sir:
Your astonishment's odd:
I am always about in the Quad,
And that's why the tree
Will continue to be,
Since observed by
Yours faithfully,
GOD

The classic Hollywood narrative convention was to present only what was essential to advance the plot. Many European and other film makers have challenged this slavish adherence to an edited construction of film time and space, restricted to the strict require-ments of a story. They moved away from the conventional limits imposed by Hollywood narrative continuity and inserted shots which had possibly no plot requirement but provided indicators of a world larger than the limitations imposed by the constraints of only follow-ing story requirements.

Yasijuro Ozu's 'Tokyo Story' (1953) inserts shots of factories and urban scenes at points in the film which appear to have no direct reference to the story. Although these locations are near where the story takes place, they do not directly connect with the story. The existence of these non-essential narrative shots appear to give greater depth to our understanding of the characters and story. In a standard 'Hollywood' narrative convention production, they would be deemed superfluous and irrelevant to the plot and eliminated from the final cut.

Limited depth and perspective indicators

The viewfinder image has limited depth indicators of overlap, size changed by movement, mass and line perspective and aerial perspective. Human perception with binocular vision allows depth and size judgements to be made by head and body movement. The perspective of the viewfinder picture can be entirely different from the impression of depth experienced by an observer beside the camera.

A personal image

The viewfinder image is a bright selected rectangle containing a portion of the field of view which is personal and specific to that camera position, lens and framing. No other individual at that location has the same visual experience as the viewfinder image unless they are sharing a video output from the camera.

Monochrome

An electronic viewfinder will produce a monochrome image with a much smaller contrast range than that experienced by human sight. This tends to provide a much simpler image than the original, eliminating colour contrasts and the emotional affect of colour and emphasizing tone, mass and the perspective of line.

A stronger sense of pattern is usually displayed by a two-dimensional viewfinder picture than is seen by human perception unless an individual has trained himself to 'see' like a camera.

The viewfinder image therefore helps in composing a picture because to some extent it accentuates certain compositional elements. A well-designed image has information included but also information that has been excluded. The frame acts as a controller of attention by limiting what is to be in shot. The edge of the frame is a frontier checkpoint and the basic advice often given to trainee cameramen is to always check the edge of the frame for unnecessary detail. With a small viewfinder image, it is not always easy to see 'border incidents' of items creeping into the frame and others sliding out. When observing a large projected image or colour picture, these fringe visual activities are immediately obvious and distracting and shift the emphasis from the main subject of the shot.

The edge of frame as a reference

Because of the strong influence of the frame edges, they tend to act as an immediate perceptual reference point to horizontal and vertical lines in the image. The camera needs to be levelled to produce horizon or equivalent lines parallel to the bottom of frame and vertical lines parallel to the side of the frame unless a canted picture is required (a Dutch tilt). If this does not happen, any camera movement will produce greater or lesser distortion of the vertical and horizontal elements.

As there is constant feedback in our biological make-up between the inner ear and eye to achieve balance and remain upright, a canted shot which displaces strong verticals can have a disturbing visual effect. Carol Reed in the 'Third Man' (1949), uses a sequence of canted shots of faces peering out of doorways and windows to create an atmosphere of suspicion and instability. This reflects the central characters uneasiness in his search through Vienna where he suspects that there are mysterious events beyond his knowledge.

In the television series 'The Franchise Affair' all the flashback sequences were shot in monochrome and canted to provide a separate identity to the main narrative. The fight sequences in 'Batman' are canted not only to reflect the style of the original comic book illustrations but to provide greater dynamics to the shot composition.

Getting into and out of the frame

Although perceptually we have an awareness of a large field of view, only a small segment can receive our full attention. It is necessary for the eye to continuously make small eye movements called 'saccades' in order to scan an object. It is similar to the eye movement necessary to examine each word of text on a page.

In the west, a page of text has a structure to allow the information to be read out in the correct sequence. Starting from the top left of the page to bottom right there is no misunderstanding the path the eye must traverse. There is no similar learnt procedure for scanning an object or image unless a deliberate perceptual route is built-in which channels the eye movement along a pre-planned path.

In order to take the eye for a 'walk' around an image there needs to be a start-point and an end-point positioned within the composition. In a shot with deep perspective indicators, a common solution is by way of a series of zigzags using a path, stream, wall, etc. which is connected to the base of the frame. This should steer the eye's attention to the principal subject and then connect up with another visual element to return the eye to the start-point. Getting into the picture requires creating one spot that immediately attracts the eye and then lead it on towards the principal subject. The 'way in' to the composition must not be too visually dominant or it will act as a competing interest to the main subject.

The positioning of small and large objects, light and shadow edges, colour connections, etc., can all act as visual guides around the image. The essential requirements are that they should lead up to and emphasize the position of the main subject before being led away for the start of a new journey. A well-designed composition will provide new visual interests for the second and possibly third circuits. If the main visual route into and out of the composition is the 'melody' of the piece, the secondary design elements can provide variation and variety on the main theme.

Strong horizontal lines form a barrier across the frame and require a visual method to 'jump' across to avoid bisecting the frame into sections. A tree or similar upright will allow the eye to move over this division of the image.

The visual exit from the composition need not be positioned at the same point as the start but can be a bright spot, for example, leading to infinity in the distance. What should be guarded against is an exit that leaves the majority of the frame unexplored. The designer of a maze intends the traveller to make a few circuits before discovering the centre and then they are allowed to search for the exit. A well-designed image has one entrance for the eye, one principal subject and then several routes to the exit. This can be accomplished with the main elements forming a pyramid, for a strong unified composition or a circle, which has the virtue, as the classical symbol of unity, of unifying and simplifying the composition. It keeps the eye within the frame. For a more dynamic composition, an irregular shape allows for eye movement which is diverse and asymmetric.

The other distraction to a well-organized visual tour is allowing the eye to get too close to the edge of the frame and then be led out by speculating on what is beyond the frame (see closed frame above).

Reading left to right

Control of eye movement on a page of text is by way of left to right scanning and by structuring the text in lines and paragraphs. The habit of reading left to right is culturally so strong that it is claimed western readers use the same left to right scan when looking at paintings, cinema and theatre. This may be a consideration when staging positions in a set up (see Chapter 5, mirror reverse).

Frame and subject size

Filling the frame with the principal subject appears, at first sight, to be an efficient way of eliminating irrelevant detail. A close shot concentrates the attention and avoids the complications of integrating other visual elements into a cohesive composition. The closer you get to the main subject, the easier it is for the viewer to understand the priorities of the shot and the quicker it is for the cameraman to find the optimum framing. The close shot is efficient in communication and often, because it only requires a small area to be designed and lit, economic in production.

There have been many successful productions that stay close almost all the time. A series of close shots builds up tension and intensity not only because of the claustrophobic impact of the tight images but also because of the absence of any visual information to assist the viewer in locating the action. Mystery and tension is enhanced if the audience is 'lost' and has no frame of reference for the events they are watching. The production style of one television series often involved starting tight on a new scene so that there was suspense and complexity for the audience in deciding where they were and what was happening. Sometimes the audience were released from their confusion by an 'explanation' shot well into the scene, but often there was no visual description of the setting, how many people were involved and their physical relationship to each other.

The composition of a close shot need not be devoid of location information. Because of the magnification of detail, a close shot may be quicker at establishing atmosphere and locality than a more general or vague wide shot. A generalization would be that a close shot intensifies the attention to detail – the viewer cannot easily overlook the visual information that is being presented. A wider shot may be used to show relationships, create atmosphere or express feeling but requires tighter design control of the composition to achieve these objectives. A wider area of view may have more visual elements, lighting, contrast, colour, etc., to integrate for visual unity, whereas a closer shot can be effective with very simple framing.

Frames within frames

Seitenverhältnis

The aspect ratio of the frame and the relationship of the subject to the edge of frame has a considerable impact on the composition of a shot. Historically, in print photography, there have been two preferred aspect ratios – the landscape format, which has a predominantly horizontal shape, and the portrait format, which emphasizes the vertical aspect ratio.

Film and television programmes usually stay with one aspect ratio for the whole production. There have been a few examples of multi-image films which either use a split screen of two, four or more separate images whilst other productions have altered the shape of the screen according to content.

One simple way of breaking up the repetition of the same projected shape and to adjust the aspect ratio to suit the content is to create compositions that involve frames within frames. The simplest device is to frame a shot through a doorway or arch which emphasize the enclosed view and down-plays the enclosing frame and wall.

By using foreground masking, an irregular 'new' frame can be created which gives variety to the constant repetition of the screen shape. A frame within a frame breaks the monotony and also provides the opportunity for compositional diversity. The familiar over-the-shoulder two shot is in effect a frame within a frame image as the back of the foreground head is redundant information and is there to allow greater attention to be focused on the speaker and the curve of the head into the shoulder gives a more visually attractive shape to the side of the frame (see Figure 1.2).

A frame within a frame emphasizes the principal subject by enclosing it with a secondary frame and often gives added depth to the shot. There are a number of ways of creating a secondary frame including the use of semi-silhouette foreground objects or windows or mirrors that divide the frame into a smaller rectangle. If this is badly done, there is the risk of creating a divided frame with equal and competing areas of interest. Strong vertical and horizontal elements can create two images which are unconnected and provide no visual direction and allow ambiguity in the viewer's mind as to which image is dominant.

The other compositional problem occurs with the relationship between the edge of frame and the frame-within-a-frame shape. If these are similar and the inside shape follows the frame line then there is simply a contraction of the screen size. Divided interest in a frame can be created by the over emphasis of visual elements that are not the principal subject or they may be indecision of what is the principal subject.

The most common example of this is the newsreader shot framed in one half of the shot and 'balanced' by a logo or generic graphic enclosed in a 'window' in the other half of the shot. The two images are usually not visually integrated and fight each other for attention. Often the newsreader appears to be uncomfortably near one edge of the frame being pushed out by the dominant position of the graphic.

It is almost impossible to achieve visual unity with a combination of presenter plus a strong graphic 'window' unless the presenter occupies at least three-quarters of the frame and can overlap the graphics window. A fifty–fifty split in the frame is often seen in news bulletins reflecting journalistic preferences formed by experiences of text page newspaper layouts.

Electronic graphics have a generous surround of 'non-action' area which is required because some domestic television sets are overscanned and the margins of the transmitted picture are not seen. Essential information such as text (name supers, telephone numbers, etc.) is automatically kept out of this border. Pictures derived from cameras have no such automatic control and can and do produce images that overlap the action area boundary. Consequently many factual programmes allow electronic graphic material to push presenters off the screen or squeeze them to the edge of the frame in composite shots.

Aspect ratio

Since the early seventies when NHK (the Japan Broadcasting Corporation) first began research into a high-definition television system, there has been a prolonged and often heated debate about what constitutes the ideal aspect ratio for television. These arguments often repeated the same concerns and advantages expressed in the earlier film industry controversies when widescreen aspect ratios were introduced.

Some proponents for the new widescreen shape suggest that it must be capable of being received on existing 4 ×3 screens. Others suggest that a totally new non-compatible HDTV system is required to take advantage of new technology.

The Pal Plus terrestrial system allows 'letterbox' viewing on 4 × 3 sets but provides 'helper' signals to improve the quality of the 16 × 9 widescreen image when displayed on a purpose-built 16 × 9 set.

As well as the arguments about the quality, economic viability and the political implications of adopting as standard one of the competing formats, there is also the need to accommodate the transmission of the back library of widescreen film production and the continuing preference for film widescreen production in aspect ratios of

Figure 4.5 Film and TV aspect ratios include: (a) 2.35:1 – 35mm anamorphic (Panavision/Cinemascope); (b) 1.85.1 – Widescreen film; (c) 1.78:1 (16:9) – Video widescreen; (d) 1.69:1 – Super 16mm; (e) 1.33:1 (4x3) – Academy ratio and TV.

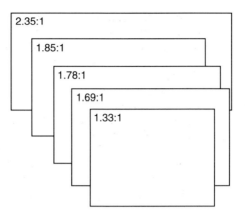

2.35:1, 1.85.1 and TV productions in 1.78:1 (16:9) and 1.69:1 (Super 16mm). There is also a huge library of film and television material shot in the ratio of 1.33:1 (4 × 3). A proposal that a 2:1 format may resolve this confusion has been suggested by the American Society of Cinematographers (Figure 4.5).

There is a further consideration in the aspect ratio debate which concerns size of screen. Someone sitting in a front row cinema seat may have as much as 58° of their field of view taken up by the screen image. This can be reduced to as little as 9.5° if he views the screen from the back row. The average television viewer typically sees a picture no wider that 9.2°.

Dr Takashi Fujio at the NHK research laboratories carried out research on viewers preference for screen size and aspect ratio and his findings largely formed the justification for the NHK HDTV parameters. The research suggests that the majority of viewers preferred a wider aspect ratio than 4:3 plus a larger screen with a corresponding increase in resolution, brightness and colour rendition. His conclusion was that maximum involvement by the viewer was achieved with a 5:3 aspect ratio viewed at 3 to 4 picture height distance. Normal viewing distance (in Japan) was 2 to 2.5 metres which suggested an ideal screen size of between 1m × 60cm and 1.5m × 90cm. With bigger room dimensions in the USA and Europe, even larger screen sizes may be desirable. Sitting closer to a smaller screen did not involve the viewer in the action in the same way.

If a mixture of formats are to be transmitted, they will be viewed with a variety of smaller or larger black bands around the image whatever format set for reception is used, or some attempt will have to be made in programme production to find compromise compositions which can be cropped (without too much aesthetic degradation) depending on the aspect ratio of the screen on which they are viewed. But this type of format compromise does inhibit good composition.

In the past, widescreen feature film compositions made no concession to the film being viewed on television. When transmitted on a 4 × 3 TV screen attempts were made to 'pan' the image to keep significant action within the transmission frame. The 'pan and scan' conversion of widescreen to 4 × 3 aspect ratio often introduced unmotivated pans following dialogue from one side of the widescreen to the other. Portions of the widescreen composition were plundered from the original shot to form new shots and this devalued the original camerawork and editing.

Widescreen enthusiasts usually suggest that the wider format is more closely akin to the human perceptual experience. As we have discussed, the eye focuses on a very small segment of the total field of view but the peripheral vision is significant in establishing location. Widescreen subject matter appears to favour exterior action or sports coverage and one of the first regular widescreen (16:9) television transmissions in the UK was horse racing on Channel 4.

The assumption that widescreen equates with spectacle is a throwback to the Hollywood attempts in the 1950s to meet the growing competition of television with 'spectacular' productions that TV could not provide. Since that period, there have been many productions which have demonstrated how effective widescreen is when shooting interiors. The 'visual fluff' at the edge of a 2.35.1 widescreen image, as one technical commentator described it, 'was unnecessary, and could always be cropped when transmitted on TV'. The implication of this thinking by vested interest eager to persuade the public to change the shape of their television sets, is that widescreen composition is simply 4:3 with a little bit of 'visual fluff' tacked on to each end of the frame.

The disturbing element in this aspect ratio debate is that frequently the technical quality and economic viability is argued in detail whereas the knock-on effects of cropping and compositional distortions are considered a side issue. The justification of widescreen in the first place was its ability to engage the audience. The practicalities of achieving a compatible widescreen/academy size television system appears to have swept past that basic point.

Widescreen

Widescreen television composition faces some of the same problems that film solved forty years ago. It is a common cliché that TV is a talking head medium but it could also be argued that this label could just as well be applied to film. Many film and television scripts require the speaker and the listener to be in the same frame. Two people talking created the mixture of close-ups, medium close-ups and over-the-shoulder two shots that form the basic shot pattern of many scenes.

Depending on shot size, the space between two speakers facing each other in mid-shot on a 4 ×3 TV is small and emphasizes their relationship. Two speakers in widescreen can have greater space between them and the shot may now emphasize their relationship not to each other, but to the background setting. Using the same type of standard shot, their physical relationship may now accidentally imply loss of contact, a breakdown of the relationship simply by the greater intervening space between them. A number of basic television shots may need to be re-thought to fit the widescreen shape.

From a cameraman's point of view, the worst compromise is a dual standard transmission where a 16:9 image is composed for viewers with the new format but the production is also watched by viewers as a cropped picture on existing 4:3 sets without 'letterboxing'.

Composition for 16:9

Shots tighter than MCU can be difficult to frame for 16:9 and the tendency is to continually tighten to lose the 'space' around the ears.

When people are being interviewed, there is an optimum distance between them where they both feel at ease. The single shot on 16:9 has the problem of avoiding being too tight and producing a 'looking through a letterbox' look whilst avoiding being too loose and getting the interviewer in shot in the 'looking space' of the interviewee. The compromise is an over-the-shoulder two shot but care must be taken in the reverse to get good continuity in body posture, etc. There needs to be greater physical separation between presenters, interviews, etc. to avoid edges of arms, shoulders creeping into the edge of the frame. This has a knock-on effect on the front-on two shot where the participants now appear to have too much space between them.

The advantage claimed for 16:9 (especially HDTV) is that the increased size of screen and the improved definition in the wide shot is so good that fewer close-ups are required. This can create its own problems in editing. Wide shots need to be sufficiently different in their distribution of similar objects to avoid jump cuts in editing. Typical bad cuts can happen with seascape horizons (yacht racing, etc.) where the yachts jump in and out of frame if the horizon is in the same position in successive shots. The same 'jump' can happen with some types of landscape. A good cut needs a change in shot size or significant change in content to be invisible.

There is the advantage of 16:9 allowing a wider shot with less sky or ground and square-on shots of buildings can replace the angled shot necessary in a 4:3 frame to include all the structure. Framing and staging (see Chapter 9) to avoid high contrast elements in the shot now have to contend with a wider shot. Many types of sports coverage also benefit from the wider aspect ratio.

Close-ups of strong vertical subjects (e.g. fingering on clarinets and saxophones) are a problem but keyboard shots are easier and 'edgy' objects on the edge of frame do not seem to be so distracting in the wide format.

1.5" Viewfinders

One of the most significant differences between normal perceptual experience and the experience of viewing an image in a viewfinder, is size. The viewfinder image is very small and therefore a condensed version of what can be perceived. The eye can quickly scan a great diversity of detail in the viewfinder image which would not be possible in the original scale. The subject is scaled down and perceptually dealt with in a different manner than the original. It is the world in miniature and looking through a viewfinder exerts the same kind of fascination that a scale model has. A model railway layout depicts a landscape capable of a single glance before allowing a detailed examination from a high angle.

HDTV has a greatly enhanced definition and a greatly increased screen size. Finding focus and the limits of focus on a 1.5" monochrome viewfinder will become more and more critical and demanding. Monochrome TV camera viewfinders are two generations behind the technology of other areas of television engineering.

Summary

At the same moment that we perceive the identity of an object within a frame, we are also aware of the spatial relationship between the object and the frame. These frame 'field' of forces exert pressure on the objects contained within the frame and all adjustment to the composition of a group of visual elements will be arranged with reference to these pressures. Different placement of the subject within the frame's 'field of forces' can therefore induce a perceptual feeling of equilibrium, of motion or of ambiguity.

The *closed frame* technique is structured to keep the attention only on the information that is contained in the shot. The *open frame* convention allows action to move in and out of the frame and does not disguise the fact that the shot is only a partial viewpoint of a much larger environment.

The perspective of the viewfinder picture can be entirely different from the impression of depth experienced by an observer beside the camera. A stronger sense of pattern is usually displayed by a two-dimensional viewfinder picture than is seen by human perception unless an individual has trained himself to 'see' like a camera. The viewfinder image therefore helps in composing a picture because to some extent it accentuates certain compositional elements.

A generalization would be that a close shot intensifies the attention to detail – the viewer cannot easily overlook the visual information that is being presented. A wider shot may be used to show relationships, create atmosphere or express feeling but requires tighter design control of the composition to achieve these objectives. A wider area of view may have more visual elements, lighting, contrast, colour, etc. to integrate for visual unity, whereas a closer shot can be effective with very simple framing.

5
Visual design

Grouping and organization

Perceptual response

There are objective principles of perception and therefore there are specific ways of organizing the visual elements within a frame to produce a predictable perceptual response.

Visual coherence is related to the inherent characteristics of perception. 'Seeing' is not simply a mechanical recording by the eye. Understanding the nature of an image is initially accomplished by the perceptual grouping of significant structural patterns. One of the aims of good composition is to find and emphasize structural patterns that the mind/eye can easily grasp.

There are a limited number of visual elements that can be seen clearly in their individual characteristics and relationships at any one time. Even this limited number of five or six distinct items is dependent on the intensity of the attention of the observer.

There is a tendency to group and organize items together to form a cluster of shapes to make up a total image that can be fully comprehended in one attentive act. Some elements are grouped together because they are close to each other. Others are bound together because they are similar in size, direction or shape (Figure 5.1).

One theory, that attempts to explain the brain/eye's tendency to group and simplify, is that the images formed by the lenses of the eyes are picked up point by point by millions of small receptor organs that are largely isolated from each other. Rudolph Arnheim in *Art and Visual Perception* suggests that the brain at the receiving end of a mosaic of millions of individual messages pieces them together by the rules of similarity and simplicity. Similar size, direction of movement or shape are instantly grouped together and a complex image can then be understood by a few clusters of shapes.

Composition must therefore aim to create a unifying relationship between the visual elements of an image in order to feed the perceptual system with patterns that can be easily assimilated by the observer.

Figure 5.1 From 'Language of Vision', Gyorgy Kepes.

'sp ati l org anisati on isthe vit alfacto rin a noptic lm essage'

'spatial organisation is the vital factor in an optical message'

Similarity by proximity

Grouping objects together because they are near to each other in the frame is the simplest method of visual organization. One of mankind's oldest examples of perceptual grouping is probably the patterns imposed on isolated and unconnected stars to form the signs of the zodiac. Grouping a foreground and a background object by proximity can achieve a coherent design in a composition.

Proximity of objects in the frame can also create relationships that are unwanted (e.g. the example of objects behind people's heads which appear on the screen as 'head wear').

Similarity of size

Same size objects in a frame will be grouped together to form one shape or pattern. The most common example of this principle is the grouping and staging of crowd scenes.

This grouping by size and proximity can be used in a reverse way to emphasize one person in a crowd scene by isolating the individual so that they cannot be visually grouped with the crowd (Figure 5.2).

Because of the assumed similarity of size between individual people, staging people in the foreground and in the background of a shot allows visual unity in the perception of similar shapes and also an effective impression of depth indicated by the diminished image size of the background figure.

Figure 5.2 Perceptual grouping by size and proximity can emphasize the 'odd one out' that does not fit the pattern. This is a straightforward compositional method of emphasizing the main subject in the frame.

Similarity by closure

Searching for coherent shapes in a complex image, human perception will look for, and if necessary, create simple shapes. The more consistent the shape of a group of visual elements the more easily it can be detached from a confusing background. Straight lines will be continued by visual projection, curved lines that almost form a circle will be mentally completed.

A popular use of this principle is the high angle shot looking down on a seething crowd moving in one direction whilst the principle figure makes a desperate journey through the crowd in the opposite direction. We are able to keep our attention on the figure because of the opposing movements and also because we mentally project their straight line movement through the crowd. The principal figure would soon be absorbed within the crowd if they frequently changed direction.

Figure 5.3 Emphasizing the main subject in the frame by lens height (a low angle puts the foreground Fred Astaire higher in the frame and the camera distance makes him much larger than the background figure).

The street lamps in the background are equidistant from the lens but because they have been designed to be progressively smaller and thinner from left to right they persuade the eye that they are receding into the distance.

Similarity of colour

Objects grouped by colour is another effective method of compositional organization. Uniforms and a team's sports wear are linked together even if they are scattered across the frame. Identical coloured dance costumes for the chorus in musicals are used to structure movement and to emphasize the principals dressed in a contrasting colour scheme. But the opposite can also be effective. In a dance sequence in 'Top Hat' (1935), Fred Astaire in white tie and tails is backed by a chorus of identically costumed male dancers. Their unity as a group is held together by proximity, size and lighting. His separation and emphasis is achieved by being in the foreground and therefore a more dominant figure and by choreography which emphasizes the principal dancer (Figure 5.3).

Visual weight

One of the problems in compiling a 'flow chart' of how the mind perceives an image is the speed at which the perceptual process functions. There are rarely discrete steps that can be listed in order as frequently the mind/eye instantaneously uses all the component parts of perception to grasp the relevance of an image. The speed at which visual information is absorbed and often unconsciously acted upon can be seen in the everyday activity of driving a car in heavy traffic or crossing a busy city street. Visual deductions, evaluations and decisions flow through the mind/eye at a rapid rate without pause to consciously analyse or deliberate on the continually changing visual 'cacophony'.

Television and film images frequently have the same complexity as a driver's view of the traffic ahead. The difficulty in describing how effective composition works is that no one ingredient acts in isolation. Each of the different groupings by shape, light/dark contrasts, line, colour, etc. can be individually part of perception or they can, depending on the content of the shot, be the dominant element.

Visual weight is the term given to the strength or impact different aspects of the image have on the overall balance of a composition.

Figure and ground

Definition

The relationship between 'figure' and 'ground' is fundamental to an understanding of perception and composition. Figure describes the shape that is immediately observable whilst ground defines that shape by giving it a context in which to exist. Figure is the prime visual element that is being communicated but can only be transmitted in a relationship with a ground (Figures 5.4a and 5.4b).

Figure need not be physically closer to the lens than ground although that part of the image that is seen as figure is often perceived as being closer to the viewer regardless of its position in the frame. Figure is usually smaller in area than ground and figure/ground cannot be seen simultaneously. They are viewed

Figure 5.4 (a)(b) Figure describes
the shape that is immediately
observable whilst ground defines
that shape by giving it a context in
which to exist. A ground can be
visually simple or complex but still
remain subservient to the figure.

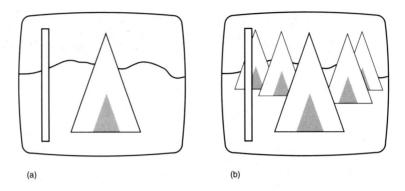

(a)   (b)

sequentially. Figure is seen as having form, contour or shape whilst
ground is seen as having none of these characteristics.

Any visual element in the frame that stands out and achieves
prominence will be considered by the observer as figure even if this
object has been assessed of no visual importance by the cameraman.
Hence the infamous background object that sits neatly on a subject's
head totally ignored by the snapshotter whose concentration is
wholly centred on what he considers is the only 'figure' in frame.
When two or more objects are grouped together they are perceived
as one 'figure' even though the cameraman may have mentally
marked out one of them as 'background'.

Figure/ground flip

A characteristic of ground is that it visually recedes and its detail is
not noticed. There may be a number of figures in a frame and the
visual elements that make up figure and ground can change their role
as attention moves from one subject to another (Figure 5.5). This is
termed figure/ground flip. The cameraman's craft is directed towards
controlling the viewer's attention on figure whilst remembering that
ground is equally important as it defines foreground. They are
separate yet they work together.

Figure/ground flip occurs when shape, tone or contour of ground
becomes more dominant or is perceived as more dominant in the
image. This can happen with a frame within a frame shot such as an

Figure 5.5 With some subjects,
there is indecision as to what is
figure and what is ground.
Figure/ground flip is when different
visual elements reverse their role.
The vase shape disappears when
two profiles are recognized.

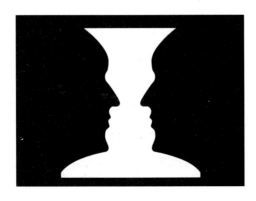

Figure 5.6 The window and the visual detail it frames functions as the figure with the interior wall as a featureless ground. If the observer's attention is allowed to switch to the interior, this is now perceived to be the figure with the window becoming the ground.

The cameraman's craft is directed towards controlling the viewer's attention on figure whilst remembering that ground is equally important as it defines foreground. They are separate yet they work together.

entrance in a wall. The entrance and the visual detail it frames functions as the figure with the wall as a featureless ground. If the observer's attention is allowed to switch to the wall which is now perceived to have texture and contrast this becomes the figure with the entrance becoming ground. The shot will quickly lose impact as the two 'figures' fight for attention (Figure 5.6).

Control

Controlling the figure/ground relationship requires emphasizing the importance of the selected figure by light, brightness, colour, differential focus, texture, position, etc. whilst removing sufficient visual detail from the ground to avoid it competing with the figure (Figure 5.7).

The use of a very narrow angle lens can blur the distinction between figure and ground. As the focal length of the lens increases, with the camera further from the subject, size relationships between objects at different distances from the lens are not so marked as in 'normal' eye perspective and all visual elements in the frame may achieve equal importance. The accompanying narrower zone of focus of objects at a great distance from the lens helps to discriminate between the intended figure and its out of focus ground.

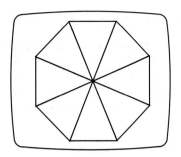

Figure 5.7 Although there are two Maltese crosses displayed, the cross whose main axes corresponds to the vertical and horizontal edges of the frame is usually selected as the figure with the other cross becoming the field. The frame edge reference is very influential in determining the subject priority.

Camouflage deliberately intends to deceive the observer in deciding what is figure and what is ground. Living creatures confuse their adversaries by attempting to 'break up' their overall shape and form by a fragmented, unsymmetrical pattern similar to their background habitat. Poor visualization by a cameraman of what is figure and what is ground in an image can achieve the same confusion.

It is easy to overestimate the psychological or narrative importance of one element when setting up a shot and underestimate its actual visual dominance within the frame. It may well have strong narrative importance but does it look visually significant? Many snapshots fail because the attention, when the photograph was taken, was wholly concentrated on one element of the field of view usually because it had strong personal significance. Even though it fails to hold the attention of a wider audience, the print may still have a strong subjective interest to one or two individuals because they will continue to ignore all but the main subject in the frame when looking at the image (see below, the section entitled Interest).

Spot/location

As discussed in Chapter 4 on Frame, the position of a small, isolated visual element within the frame will achieve dominance depending on its relationship to the frame edge, the nature of its background and its contrast to its background. Its location within the frame will depend on its movement or implied movement (e.g. direction of eye line). If the subject is offset on one of the intersections of thirds (see Intersection of Thirds in Chapter 8) it can achieve compositional balance by its perceived direction moving into the frame. A more dynamic and dissonant arrangement is created by an off-centre location with movement towards the nearest edge of frame.

Usually a dead centre framing drains the shot of any visual interest as there is no dynamic tension between the subject and the frame. Likewise a very eccentric positioning close to the edge of the frame requires some compositional reason provided by the nature of the subject or its background.

Contrast with background is also a compositional consideration either in colour, brightness level or texture to achieve pictorial unity.

Shape

Definition of shape

One of the basic Gestalt theories of perception is that we tend to simplify visual patterns as much as the image will allow in order to grasp the significance of the image. The shape or outside boundary of an object is perceived as one dimensional even though our knowledge and experience of the world demonstrates that the majority of objects exist in three dimensions.

This outside boundary, the shape of an object, plays a significant part in visual composition because of the ease and speed of grasping its simple pattern and relationships. If shapes become too abstract and ambiguous, however, then, as the wide variety of responses to the same Rorschach ink blob test demonstrates, individual states of mind and memory will control interpretation.

Simplicity and economy have always been valued in visual communication in the search to reduce to essentials in order to clearly communicate. Shape is a simple, visually easily 'digestible' element in a composition and when setting up a shot, a few similar shapes should be looked for which can be grouped and reinforce the overall impact of the image.

Grouping visual elements by overall shape

Similar shape is an effective way of unifying an image in order to make it easily comprehensible. The three basic regular shapes of oval, triangle and circle can be used in a variety of ways such as in the grouping of people or objects. A shot can be strengthened if the visual elements are structured so that the eye follows one of the basic shapes around the frame. Triangle and oval forms are the most flexible and accommodating in enclosing shapes and many cameramen when they run their eye around a potential shot are seeking this kind of relational shape to bind the composition together.

The overall shape of a composition also indicates mood or character. The triangle with a broad base is considered to have strength and stability. A popular, if unconscious reflection of this is the shot of the newsreader who sits with elbows on the news desk making a 'trustworthy' triangle.

The triangle is a very flexible shape as a design element in a composition. The cameraman can control the shape and impact of a triangle by choice of lens-angle, camera distance and height. The line convergence forming the boundary of a triangle within a composition can be altered and arranged to provide the precise control of the compositional elements.

The ability to analyse shapes in an image rather than simply seeing the content is an essential step in developing an eye for composition. If there appears to be a lack of unity in the image and if the main subject appears to be fighting the background then it is more than likely that an overall leading shape line around the frame is missing. Search for background shapes or re-light for background shapes that will connect and relate to foreground.

Light/dark relationships

Proximity, area and contrast

Every element in an image has a specific brightness. One area will be seen as bright, another will be perceived as dark. The visual 'weight' of different brightness levels will depend on proximity, area and contrast. The eye is naturally attracted to the highlight areas in a frame but the contrast and impact of an object's brightness in the frame will depend on the adjacent brightness levels. A shot of a polar bear against snow will require different compositional treatment than a polar bear in a zoo enclosure. A small bright object against a dark background will have as much visual weight in attracting the eye as a large bright object against a bright background. The relationship between different brightness levels in the frame play an important part in balancing the composition. The study of light and dark in composition is termed chiaroscuro – Italian for 'obscure light'.

For John Alton, the definitive Hollywood cameraman of the *Film Noir* genre, black was the most important element in the shot. The most important lamps for him were the ones he did not turn on. The control and distribution of light in composition will be discussed in more detail in the chapter on light and lighting but it is worth emphasizing here that the relationship between the light and dark areas of the frame play a critical role in many interior and exterior shots. A large amount of black can be balanced with a small highlight deftly positioned. The high key/low key mood of the frame will dictate styles of composition as well as atmosphere. A few strong light/black contrasts can provide very effective visual designs.

There is a reduction in the overall contrast range that can be reproduced in a visual medium but the depiction of strong contrasts can still be achieved by the use of light/dark comparisons.

Strong contrast creates a solid separation and good figure/ground definition. When size is equal, the light/dark relationship plays an essential part in deciphering which is figure and which is ground. Equal areas of light and dark can be perceived as either figure or ground.

The boundary area of a shape often relies on a light/dark relationship. A figure can be separated from its background by backlighting its edge. A highlight in the frame will attract the eye and if it is not compositionally connected to the main subject of interest, it will compete and divert the attention.

Line

Line is a powerful picture making design component and can be used to structure the attention of the observer. Within the frame, any visual elements that can be perceptually grouped into lines can be used to direct the eye around the image from one part of the picture to another to end, preferably, on the main subject of interest. Attention is attracted to where two lines cross or one line abruptly changes direction. The eye is attracted to the point of convergence of the lines or the implied point of crossing. In practice, a line need not be visible to act as a strong compositional element but it can be implied such as the line of a person's gaze.

The vertical line

An isolated vertical subject such as a tree or a tower has directness and rigidity. It is immediately seen and takes visual precedence over any horizontal or other lines in the frame. The human figure in a landscape immediately attracts attention not only because of its psychological importance but because of this vertical aspect. It has been suggested that an image consisting of strong vertical elements can convey dignity, solemnity and serenity.

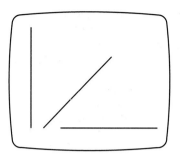

Figure 5.8 An upright line appears balanced, a diagonal line implies movement and a horizontal line is at rest.

Figure 5.9 Lines of convergence can be placed to have as their focus the dominant subject in the frame. Strong pictorial lines can be controlled by lens position to lead to and emphasize the main subject.

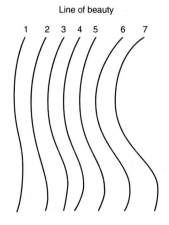

Figure 5.10 Line number 4 was considered by Hogarth to have the most attractive shape.

The strength of a vertical visual element in a composition means that some kind of design elements have to be introduced to establish image unity. Usually a vertical line requires a horizontal element to cross it at some point in order to achieve a satisfactory composition. If a vertical line simply divides the frame, two disconnected images will be created – a split screen. The most common use of the vertical line is to link two competing areas of the picture to achieve unity. This could be a carefully positioned tree to connect landscape with sky or a strong vertical line in a piece of furniture or architecture to link the lower half of the frame with the top. This vertical element should have its greater proportion in what is being established as the dominant area or subject of the picture.

The leaning line

Diagonal arrangements of lines in a composition produce a greater impression of vitality than either vertical or horizontal lines. A line is most active when it runs from corner to corner. A tree before it is felled is a line that is vertical and stable. From the moment it is cut down it begins its journey to becoming a horizontal line and static. Its most potent and active angle as a line is at 45° where its rush to 'rest' is most keenly anticipated. A line at an angle is perceptually seen as a line that is in motion unless it is so marginally off vertical it could be simply the result of camera set-up. Compositions with a strong diagonal element imply movement or vitality (Figure 5.8).

Convergence of lines

As we have seen, the distance from lens to subject, lens-angle and camera height are a decisive influence on the convergence of lines within a frame. Lines of convergence can be placed to have as their focus the dominant subject in the frame. Strong pictorial lines can be controlled by lens position to lead to and emphasize the main subject (Figure 5.9).

Line of beauty

William Hogarth identified seven different curved lines and picked out one of these as the most perfect 'line of beauty'. It is similar in shape to the line of a woman's back and has been dubbed the 'S' curve. It occurs frequently in Michelangelo's paintings and is seen in natural form in such things as wind-swept arable crops and the upward swirl of flames (Figure 5.10).

Curves

One of the useful compositional uses of curved lines in an image is to guide the eye to the main point of interest. A straight line takes the eye immediately from point A to point B. A curve can move the eye around the frame in a less direct movement and knit disparate elements together on the way. A curve has the advantage of being a progressive change of direction which allows a softer visual movement around an image compared to the zigzag pinball movement of straight lines. Also, unlike straight lines, curves do not interact with the edge of frame either in direction or by comparison.

Rivers, roads, the line of a hill or hedge, banister rails, etc. can all be used to rhythmically knit a composition together. Where curves can be duplicated and repeated in different sizes, then not only will a great deal of visual interest be set up, but the spaces between objects enclosed by the boundary lines of the curved shapes have a greater visual interest. The 'ground' to the image will have greater vitality even though it will still act as an anchor to the overall design.

The strength of a composition created by curves can be increased by an all-over pattern across the frame and by the strong contrast of light and shade. Shadows of foliage, decorative wrought iron railings, grilles and blinds, etc. will provide pattern. Even straight line shadows such as sunlight through Venetian blinds falling on a curved surface can provide another source of controlled pattern and curve in the frame. Curves can also be implied by repetition of the same type of object and this effect can be emphasized by the use of a long lens.

A curved lead-in line to the main subject of interest has always been one of the most common techniques to get the observer into the frame and then out again. There is often an inclination to try to avoid such a clichéd technique but the perceptual experience is that it is effective, that it holds and guides the attention of the viewer and that alternative 'lead-in' devices can just as quickly become visually devalued and stale.

Using foreground curved shapes to mask off part of the picture to produce a frame within a frame is often employed to break up a series of rectangle compositions. As previously mentioned, the classic tight over-the-shoulder blanking off the side of the frame by a silhouette head and part of the shoulder is a simple way of achieving a new frame outline.

Rhythm and visual beat

Rhythm and pattern describe two aspects of a linked series of visual elements. Pattern can be defined as a design or figure repeated across the frame such as bricks in a wall viewed from a square-on position. A wallpaper design may have a repetition of a few shapes which is repeated indefinitely.

Rhythm, whilst occurring in pattern, can also be present without repetition. Visual rhythm can occur in the relationship between a series of shapes or lines such as a crabbing shot which has foreground objects wiping across the frame. These may be equally spaced such as columns (pattern) or irregularly spaced but still forming a relationship.

Musical rhythm developing over time would appear to be quite different from the experience of perception where it is often assumed that an understanding of an image is grasped instantaneously. But the mind/eye moving over a series of visual accents in an image can respond in a similar way as the mind/ear experiences listening to a series of rhythmic accents. If a connected series of visual accents are present in the image, then it can be said that a visual beat has been established. Sunlight modulated by a row of trees falling on a car travelling along a road will produce a rhythm of pattern and light. The repetitive pitch of a boat will create a regular sweep of light through a porthole onto a cabin wall. Both of these examples are created by movement but static pattern and rhythm exist in nature (the structure of petals in a flower, desert sand formations) and in man-made objects (bridge girders, field patterns, motorway junctions).

The eye readily follows a line or curve in an image and is correspondingly affected by any repetition of direction or movement of lines or shapes it is led on to. It is the transition between repetition of line and shape that sets up the rhythm of the image and by implication can be extended by the eye/mind to continue outside of the frame. Rhythm needs direction and flow and is strongest when it coincides with the natural eye-scan movement from left to right.

Repetition of camera movement can set up a visual rhythm such as crabbing across a series of foreground objects as mentioned above, or a series of zooms or tracking shots towards a subject which is identically paced. This is often used in dream or fantasy sequences to create an atmosphere of movement without end. Rhythm can express conflict, serenity or confusion and has a strong impact on the front plane composition.

Pattern

Repetition of pattern

Pattern was defined as a design or figure repeated indefinitely. Visually it is strongest if the repetition can occur across the whole of the frame and if the repetition includes a large number of the repeated shapes.

Static pattern in a composition can be uninteresting in the same way that over emphasis on symmetry becomes flat and stale. A shot of a building that has regular windows patterned across the frame will have little impact because the pattern is the centre of interest and unless a second element is introduced to act as a dissonance or counterpoint to the pattern (e.g. shadows or camera angle, etc.) the composition may not sustain attention.

Moving patterns, however, can create interest and involvement if compositional control of the image is understood. Repetition or pattern may be present in the normal field of view but the observer may be unaware of it. Placing a frame around a portion of the field of view will isolate and emphasize the repetition.

Creating patterns

For example, a shot of a pavement crowded with shoppers with a camera position looking along the pavement using a 25° lens will result in a continuous change of subject moving towards and away from the camera. Patterns of people will be created but it will be difficult for the viewer to focus on any one element. Random movement is difficult to observe and to enjoy. There is no centre of interest and no one object to contrast and compare with another. The pattern of the people is changing too rapidly.

To control pattern, frame a similar shot of the shoppers but this time use a long lens of 5° or under to create a pattern of people who stay longer in frame and therefore allow a pattern relationship to be set up. Creating repetition of equally sized shapes by the use of a long lens creates multiple appearances of similar objects which, because of camera distance, stay longer in frame.

This is because – as we discovered in the discussion on the perspective of mass – the image size relationship of subjects in shot will depend upon the camera distance from the objects. If similar sized subjects such as people are walking towards camera or away from camera at a distance (e.g. 100 m) and are framed using the narrow end of the zoom (e.g. 5° or under) the effect will be of little or no change in subject size coupled with a lack of anticipated movement. Because of the distance of the camera from the subject, there is not the anticipated change in subject size usually experienced when people walk to or away from an observer. Movement without changing size is the equivalent of running on the spot and creates the surreal dream-like quality of flight without escape.

Making patterns out of people dehumanizes them because it robs them of personality. It makes crowds into abstract statements. This type of composition is frequently used when a voice-over narration is discussing changes in inflation or shopping habits, etc. It is very difficult to find shots to illustrate abstract concepts such as 'inflation' or 'devaluation', topics that often require news footage.

Shots of cars, rooftops, a portion of a mass production process (e.g. bottles moving on a conveyor belt) can be used to create similar abstract patterns. A repetition of the same shape which either moves across the frame in a regular rhythm (e.g. the bottle) or is held within the frame for a longer period than is normally experienced by the use of a long lens compressing space, can provide attractive decorative images. They are created by camera distance, lens-angle and the movement of the subject towards or away from the lens.

Interest

Possibly the strongest design element that can be used in a composition to capture attention is for the content to have a strong emotional or psychological connection with the viewer. Either the subject of the shot has a personal association or it features a familiar human experience.

The personal connection can simply be a photo of a location, someone known to the viewer or a loved person. Millions of snapshots are treasured not for any intrinsic photographic values but because of the innate interest of their subject. This does not prevent a photo having a strong subjective interest and also having qualities which would appeal to a 'disinterested' observer with no involvement with the subject. Home videos of domestic or holiday topics can be shot so that they have a much wider appeal beyond their participants or their friends. The usual weakness of home movies is their inability to separate subjective interest from the considerations of structure and design. The content of the video dominates its form.

The most extreme examples of identification are life-threatening situations created by fictional or factual events. It is often puzzling to lay people that professional photographers in war zones or those covering civil catastrophes can still instinctively frame up and find the right angle of view to make 'decorative' images. They can still pay attention to technique, to the mechanics of recording the image, whilst the content would appear to be so overpowering that any normal feeling person would wish to intervene or help.

The separation of content, whatever its personal implications, and the technique needed to record it is part of the professional character of anyone who aspires to cover highly emotional factual situations. Many people do not have, or wish to have, the detachment necessary to keep filming when people are in extreme distress or danger. But even in less life-threatening situations, the ability not to be involved in order to stand back and, with professional detachment, consider the visual potential of an event, is essential.

The personal significance of the content of a shot will always be the most powerful design element in attracting attention but by its presentation (compositional design) its appeal can be broadened to involve and engage a much wider audience.

Direction

Within the frame there may be a visual element which produces a strong sense of visual movement. A row of poplar trees or a wall for example may produce a line which creates a dominant line of movement – a visual direction which is difficult to ignore.

This strong sense of movement can either be built into the composition and provide a leading line to the main subject or it can be balanced against other movement or mass to tone it down or reduce its impact. As we have seen, diagonal lines are the most active within the frame and in particular, diagonal converging lines pull the eye like a signpost arrow.

These direction indicators pick up the eye and carry it across or around the frame. There must be a resolution to a vigorous movement of directional lines or the composition will be perceived as lacking an essential element. It is similar to a pan which sets up expectation as it moves to a conclusion only to disappoint if the end image is uninteresting. A strong directional line that leads nowhere in the frame is a frustrated journey.

Colour

Colour as a design element is such a powerful force that it requires a separate discussion (see Chapter 7).

Balance

Visual reorganization

Due to the effect of perceptual 'reorganization', no visual element can exist in isolation within the frame. Within the act of perception,

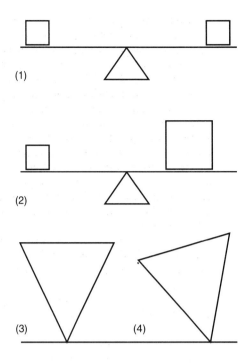

the eye/mind groups and forms relationships of the shapes it has
organized.

One relationship is balance – the relative visual weight of one
clump of visual elements compared to another and their individual
relationships to the whole.

A technological definition of balance is the state of a body in
which the forces that act upon it compensate each other. Cameramen
will know that when they mount a large lens on the camera there is
the need to pull the body of the camera back on the pan/tilt head
until the point of balance has been achieved – the seesaw principle
where a small child at the extreme end can be balanced by an adult
sitting opposite but much closer to the pivot point. There is also
another aspect of balance connected with a combined group of
objects such as lens, matte box, camera, pan bar, viewfinder, etc.
which is connected to their overall centre of gravity and the physical position of that point of balance. This is the centre of balance of
the combined mass (Figure 5.11).

Balance in a composition is the distribution of the visual elements
across the frame so that a state of equilibrium is achieved for the
whole. Equilibrium need not mean at rest for, as in the seesaw
analogy, balance can still allow movement and therefore visual interest.

As with a camera mass, a visual pattern has a centre around which
the visual elements are grouped. The pivot point need not be and
frequently is not the centre of the frame. Balance can be achieved
by visual weight determined by size, shape (regular shape is heavier
than an irregular shape), colour, light/dark relationships, isolation of
a pictorial element, direction and the intrinsic interest of content
(e.g. the observer's wishes and fears induced by the image which may

outweigh any perceptual considerations of balance – for many people, a snake moving in any part of the frame will capture their attention irrespective of any other compositional design).

The content or intention of the image will determine which type of visual weight will be chosen to be pictorially reorganized in the process of composition. Balance helps meaning to be made visible.

The two factors that determine balance are visual weight and the direction of movement of the visual pattern. Visual weight is conditioned by its position in the frame. A visual element at the centre or close to the centre vertical axis has less weight than one at the edge of the composition. An object higher in the frame is heavier than the same size object in the lower part of the frame. An object in the right of the frame will have less compositional weight than if it was positioned in the left of the frame (see Chapter 4, Reading the frame left to right).

Similar to the seesaw principle, visual weight increases proportionally the further it is from its point of balance. A small significant object in the background will balance out a larger object in the foreground.

The resolution of balance in a composition therefore requires small to be weighted against large with reference to the centre and outside edges of the frame in order to achieve unity of the total image. A small 'weight' in the composition can be placed a long way from the centre if a balancing 'large weight' is placed close to the centre.

'Weight' need not only be differences in the physical size of balancing visual elements. Balance can be resolved with line, mass, light/dark, colour, etc.

Formal balance

Many examples are seen in religious art of figures grouped either side of the main subject. Balance is achieved by equal weighting on both sides of the frame. Although formal balance emphasizes the main central subject's importance, its symmetrical solemnity precludes visual excitement. Another form of classical balance is by the use of the Golden Mean (see Chapter 8, Compositional influences).

To hold visual attention, it is necessary to provide greater visual complexity. A formal central grouping of figures balanced around the centre of the frame although assimilated instantly fails to provoke further curiosity. Once the eye has swept around the central shape it has visually 'consumed' all that has been provided. To entice the eye to take a second tour, less obvious visual relationships need to be discovered. The eye and mind must be fed with visual variations embedded within the basic dominant pattern although it must always be remembered that the eye takes the visual path of least resistance. Unravelling a very complex set of visual variations may mean a 'switch off' for the majority until easier shots come along. But visual variety provides the stimulation necessary for holding the attention.

Dynamic balancing

Finding a dynamic balance requires not only positioning small with large or light with dark, etc., but also finding linking patterns to the main balancing duality.

Our experience of the physical properties of objects provides us with the knowledge that an object that is very large at the top and tapers to a very small base is likely to be unstable and easily toppled. The equivalent visual weight is attached to a large object at the top of the frame and a smaller object at the base. The composition appears to be unstable and transient.

Dissonance

Whereas a balanced composition aims to promote a sense of equilibrium or stability achieved, dissonance in a compositional grouping induces a feeling of discord or of resolution still to be realized.

Effective dissonance in music is not created (except by accident) by a non-musician aimlessly pressing groups of notes on a piano. It is based on the application of the theory of harmony. Dissonance in visual composition requires the same understanding of technique in order to achieve controlled disharmony.

For many centuries, the aim of composition in western painting was to weld all the elements of the painting into a pictorial unity – to achieve balance. The concept of dissonance – to deliberately offset compositional elements in order to create visual tension, only entered compositional technique to any extent in the nineteenth century.

With the advent of 'snapshot' photography in the 1860s when exposures of 1/50th second were possible, many artists were influenced by the random photographic compositions created by people in motion. Degas was one of the first artists to use 'decentralized' compositions with the main subject offset to the edge of the frame (see Figure 8.3).

A new pictorial convention arose of cutting off part of an object by the frame to imply that the action continued outside the frame. If the observer is led out of the picture frame, an expectation or curiosity in the viewer is set up, which is not satisfied by the framed image. The composition is unresolved. It is similar to the sound of one shoe dropped in the room above. There is a pause, an anticipation of the fall of the second shoe which fails to be resolved if the expected event does not occur (see the discussion of open/closed frame in Chapter 4, A hard cutoff).

Dissonant compositions are therefore deliberately structured to evoke a sense of incompleteness. Just as there is a strong wish to straighten a picture hung crookedly on a wall, a well-structured 'dissonant' shot will evoke the same feeling of a composition seeking to achieve balance. The friction and conflict that is set up can convey a strong sense of unresolved tension as well as creating interest and involvement (Figure 5.12).

Dissonant arrangement of subject matter creates a dynamic tension. But increasing the degree of unbalance to an extreme might collapse into visual anarchy and produce a composition of random items that have no relationship.

A shelf with a central object such as a clock flanked by two candlesticks can be arranged symmetrically and provide a balanced but stale arrangement. If the clock is moved towards one of the candlesticks a dissonance is set up which may make the image stronger and more interesting because of the visual inclination to return the objects to a symmetrical balance.

Figure 5.12 Dissonance in a compositional grouping induces a feeling of discord. The offset framing and the eye-line out of frame unbalances the shot and sets up a sense of visual disquiet.

Dissonance is as necessary to good composition as balance. Offsetting balance creates interest. Achieving balance can satisfy the urge for symmetry but quickly becomes uninteresting. If balance is a full stomach then dissonance is an appetite that needs to be satisfied.

Divided interest

A composition with divided interest, where the eye flicks back and forth between two equal subjects, is a composition without balance. One subject must be made subservient to the other by placement, size, focus, colour or contrast.

Sound is another design element to restore balance as viewer attention will always be directed to the source of dialogue or other sound produced by one of the competing subjects within the frame.

Visual attention can always be captured by movement. Independent of the usual compositional controlling visual elements such as brightness, mass or colour, human perception is invariably attracted by movement. At one stage in human history, survival may have relied on instantly being aware of change in the environment and movement indicates change. It may have tilted the balance between successfully gathering food or being gathered as food. Movement within the frame usually takes precedence over all other compositional devices in attracting attention.

Mirror reverse/stage left

It has often been demonstrated with western art that images are habitually scanned from left to right – the normal reading process. Theatre staging often takes account of this fact in the knowledge that the audience will automatically look to the left, the 'strong' side of the stage, as the curtain rises. Another consequence of a 'left/right'

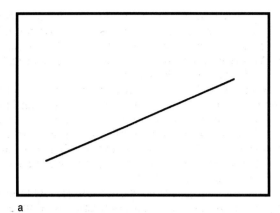 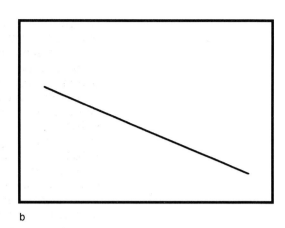

a   b

Figure 5.13 Because of the western tradition of scanning text from left to right, the movement of the line in (a) appears to be travelling uphill whereas the movement of the line in (b) appears to be going downhill.

bias is that many formal balanced compositions can be destroyed if mirror reversed (Figures 5.13a and 5.13b).

The normal scanning of an image from left to right appears to give less weight to an object on the left than if it is placed on the right of the frame. A theatrical convention of the 'strong' left side and 'weak' right side is that traditionally the Faery Queen enters stage left whilst the Demon King enters prompt side. Was there any evidence in Westerns that 'white hats' (goodies) and 'black hats' (baddies) followed this convention when entering frame or did movement continuity demands eliminate this convention in the early days of the cinema?

Balance and ambiguity

Balance is a means of eliminating ambiguity and visual confusion. Without visual organization, the message becomes confused as the observer is stuck with a visual hypothesis with insufficient information to form a conclusion.

But a visual intention to confuse, discomfort or even disorientate the viewer also has a pedigree in mass entertainment. It was popular in television in 1960s pop programmes where flashing lights, star filters and extreme flare degraded the image to produce an impression of the atmosphere of a club. Later, pop promotions, with a great deal of post-production work, elaborated this style and aimed to tease and invoke visual excitement by a string of unstructured shots, subliminal cuts and multi-images. Exploiting changes in technology, youth programmes in the 1980s used continuously moving hand-held cameras overlaid with moving graphics in an attempt to emulate the rave experience of a 'drug' induced buzz of disorientating images. As very little information could be assimilated with such a confusion of images, the style was the content that was being communicated.

Scale

A great deal of our understanding of the physical nature of the world around us is achieved by comparison of size. We often achieve recognition of an object by its proportions and its normal size relationship with other objects. A ten-foot-high shirt button would require a moment to categorize before we had established a new frame of reference. Whereas it would be instantly recognized as a button if it was at the size we normally see it.

A frame around an image seals off most of its frame of reference and can cause problems in recognition unless it is a very familiar object such as the human face or figure. Most people have been visually tricked by a close shot of a model replica when the camera pulls back to reveal it is as a fraction of the size of the original. Some objects need to be set in context in order to visually communicate clearly without any confusion of their identity.

A composition can achieve an impact by introducing an indication of scale or size comparison. It may be simply contrasting one subject with another – a small child in a large space or an ocean liner being pulled by a small tug. Viewers unfamiliar with the subject depicted may need some indication of size by comparison with a known object.

The human figure is the most easily recognized and most often used in size comparisons. An over-used technique is the familiar zoom out from a presenter to reveal that he or she is located at the top of an enormous bridge, building or natural feature. This shows scale but requires a great deal of 'dead' visual between the start and the end of the shot which are the only two images that are being compared.

More attractive compositions can be achieved by using a high angle position looking down, for example, into a valley to see a winding road with a vehicle moving along it or a train puffing through the hills. This type of image appeals to most people's general fascination with model layouts where the spectator can take up a detached position and observe a scene without being part of it.

The proximity of one subject to another allows a frame of reference to be established and associations and comparisons to be made. The same factors are at work over time with adjacent shots allowing a development of new information or continuity in story telling. Proximity of subject allows judgements of scale and connections. Proximity in time allows continuity and the relationship between visual references which constructs an argument.

Whereas the cinema image is viewed in near darkness with no visible object surrounding the screen, the television image is always in proximity with the objects surrounding the TV set. The moving image on the screen holds the attention against the surrounding competition of wallpaper, furniture, ornaments and people. The combined two-dimensional designed composition including scale indicators has now to contend, when viewed, with a three-dimensional environment.

Abstraction

The main theories of the psychology of perception are based on the concept of the perceptual process being an active exploration of form and structure to achieve recognition. Recognition usually involves categorizing and naming the object or process. Perceptual exploration involves assessing the abstract elements of the image such as shape, colour, brightness points, contrast, texture, movement and spatial position.

Recognition by establishing patterns, and grouping by similar shapes, etc., appears to play an important part in the interrogation and exploration of the visual world. Pattern and form can be abstracted from any complex subject and depicted as an image, independent of normal object recognition. An abstract image can therefore be defined as form and colour independent of subject. It is form without a figurative content and is often created by eliminating or limiting the contrast between figure and ground.

An abstract image can also be achieved by simplification. A shot of undulating sand on the sea shore will have form, texture and contrast but will have an all-over pattern across the frame that binds the composition together.

Reducing or eliminating depth indicators often results in a greater abstract element in a design. Without space or depth in a shot, form and design are concentrated in a two-dimensional pattern. This is often seen in shots of reflections and subjects with strong texture.

Although film and television camerawork often aspires to be unequivocally factual and realistic, the images are displayed on a flat screen. This two-dimensional representation often reveals abstract designs in the most mundane subjects. Long lenses or a narrow zone of focus emphasize form and shape; elimination or reduction of depth indicators, interaction between figure and ground, simplification and the over-all repetition of similar shapes all tend towards creating abstract pattern and the basic building blocks of the perceptual process.

Understanding an image

The viewer can only see the image that is selected and presented to them. Of all the thousands of images that could be filmed and recorded on any one subject, the choice of what is presented is whittled down to a few hundred. Those few images are considered to be the most economical way of visually presenting the message to be communicated. It is obviously assumed and hoped that the selected shots will be understood only in terms of the intention of their originators. A verbal instruction of 'Please close the door' would obviously be seen to have been a failed communication if a window was closed instead. How can anyone framing up a shot be certain that the viewer's understanding of the image will be identical to their own?

People's hopes, wishes, fears and personal viewpoint play a major part in their perception. If one person is terrified of spiders, any small scrap of material that is blown across the floor may invoke unreasoned anxiety. The same 'misreading' of visual images occurs especially if they set up associations with opinions strongly held. Our perception or appreciation of an image depends upon our own way of seeing.

One solution to avoid visual misunderstanding or 'misreading' of an image is the use of stereotypes. There is a huge repertoire of stereotype images usually related to the seasons of the years or rites of passage. They are sometimes impossible to resist if a story requires, for example, an indication of Christmas. There are a dozen or more well-used visual clichés that can instantly be used to communicate 'Christmas'. Offsetting the colour balance to get blue exteriors and warm welcoming yellow, interior lit windows, star filters for Christmas lights, parcels under the tree, instantly establish atmosphere and setting. The problem with such visual clichés is that they are all but drained of their impact. They are simply references to previous well-used images and are therefore instantly recognized and instantly consumed. They lack any visual development or attention sustaining design.

There are other visual stereotypes such as images of gender, race or religion that may be pressed into service unexamined by the cameraman. Roland Barthes (1973) labels these visual symbols as 'mythic'. Not in the sense of being mythologies, fairy stories or false but having the well-used appearance of being 'natural' or 'common sense'. They are the unexamined prejudgements and assumptions about life nurtured by a specific cultural background that find expression when a image is sought to express an attitude or idea. A newsreel sequence may feature angry or violent people in a street demonstration because the cameraman was briefed to search for shots containing 'action' to illustrate the event. He or she may have ignored thousands of inactive protesters as lacking 'visual' interest.

Shots may express indicators of attitude or feeling which are unconsciously understood by the viewer. A shot behind a row of prison bars looking out will evoke a different response to a shot looking through the bars into a cell. The shot has conditioned or positioned the viewpoint of the viewer to be either as a prisoner or as a visitor to the prison.

Reference by association is common in commercials where images are carefully manufactured to make a connection between a product and a result. For example, a shampoo bottle and glamorous hair are so co-joined in the same shot as to render it impossible not to draw the conclusion that one leads to the other. There is a density of visual themes which imply rather than state overtly their commercial message. The most common visual theme implies that if you are able to buy this product you will be lovable. If you cannot buy it, you will be less lovable.

The viewer, when searching for the best explanation of the available visual information, may add their own interpretation whilst being unaware of the hidden visual message they are absorbing.

Figure 5.14 The student standing in front of an approaching tank in Tiannemen Square is recycled as a symbolic image independent of the specific event recorded. (© 1989 Cable News Network Inc. All rights reserved.)

Often, a film or television image is not simply a record of an event but becomes an event in itself. The image is then used to symbolize a process or condition. The student standing in front of an approaching tank in Tiannemen Square (Figure 5.14), the street execution of a kneeling enemy prisoner, a young person engulfed in flames running towards the camera are images that have implications beyond the horrific action portrayed. They continue to be recycled as symbolic images or icons rather than existing as the specific event recorded.

Emphasizing the most important element

What is the 'best' viewpoint?

Composition involves drawing attention to the main subject and then making it meaningful. Whereas a painter needs to work on every part of the frame and to consider every part of the frame, a shot can be selected on a visual decision which ignores all but one part of the image. The poor compositional relationship between this area and the total frame may only become apparent after the event has been recorded. One of the more obvious mistakes therefore is not to see the whole picture but only that part which has initially attracted interest.

There is a puzzling piece of advice about camerawork that urges all students to 'Look before you see'. In essence this simply means to look at the overall image, and at its underlying pattern before concentrating too much on the main subject. Developing a photographic eye is giving attention to all visual elements within the field of view and not simply selecting those elements that initially attract attention. With experience comes the ability to visualize the appearance of a shot wherever the lens is positioned, without the need to continually move the camera in order to look through the viewfinder to find out what the shot will look like.

Before deciding camera position, lens-angle, framing, lighting, etc. it is worth considering the following questions.

1   What is the purpose of the shot?
2   Is the shot fact or feeling? Will the image attempt to be factual and objective and allow the viewer to draw their own conclusions or is it the intention to persuade or create an atmosphere by careful selection?
3   In what context will the shot be seen? What precedes – what follows?
4   What will be the most important visual element in the shot?

The best viewpoint is the lens position in space that emphasizes the main subject. Make certain that the eye is attracted to the part of the frame that is significant and avoid conflict with other elements in the frame (Figures 5.15a–5.15e).

To emphasize the most important element, use subject size, position, selective focus, colour, brightness and relationship to background to focus attention. Use either contrast of tone, colour

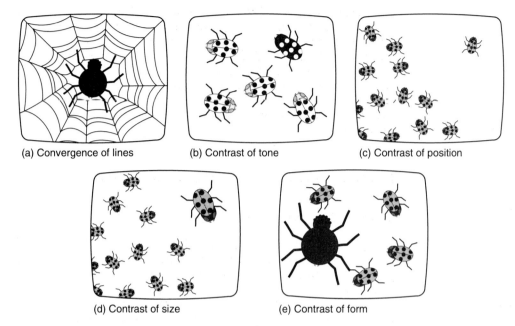

(a) Convergence of lines   (b) Contrast of tone   (c) Contrast of position

(d) Contrast of size   (e) Contrast of form

Figure 5.15 Five ways of concentrating attention on the main subject in the frame: (a) Convergence of background lines; (b) contrast of tone; (c) contrast of position; (d) contrast of size; (e) contrast of form.

and form to stress the differences between graphic elements in the shot and to balance out active relationships between opposed elements. Check that:

1   the purpose of the shot is understood;
2   the main subject is identified;
3   the camera parameters (lens position, angle, height, etc.) are positioned to emphasize the principal interest;
4   leading lines are used to point to the main subject;
5   supporting visual interest within the frame is examined and that, by careful framing and lens position, their support for the main subject is maximized and that competing areas of interest are eliminated or subdued (offset the dominant interest and balance this with a less important element);
6   principal information avoids corners and attention is kept within the picture space;
7   the image is simplified if possible by reducing to essentials.

Taking the eye for a walk

Emphasizing the main subject involves control of the eye movement across the frame. The eye travels the line of least resistance and in its movement around the frame it is similar to a pin-ball bouncing off different obstacles before being forced by the designer of the composition to end up at the main subject of interest. An interesting composition allows the eye movement moments of repose and this stop/start journey creates visual rhythm. The strongest rhythms, as we have seen, occur in patterns. Organization of the image requires the eye to be shown new unsuspected spatial relationships between similar shapes, similar tone, texture or colour.

Fill the frame if possible with interest and avoid large plain areas that are there simply because of the aspect ratio of the screen. If necessary, mask off part of the frame with a feature in the shot to give a more interesting composition and to emphasize the most important element in the frame.

Creating a front surface design

For an image to hold our attention relationships within the frame must be constantly changing. This can be achieved by movement or sound (e.g. dialogue flip-flopping between actors). It can be achieved by skilful compositional elements that lead the eye around the frame finding new patterns or visual contrasts or it can be achieved by having an involving and agreeable front surface pattern.

There is often an attempt to compensate for the loss of the third dimension in a film or television image by introducing a string of depth indicators that draws the eye into the picture. Space and the depiction of depth can provide visual interest but so can pattern. The screen on which the image is reproduced is a flat two-dimensional plane and, as we have seen with the structural skeleton of the shot and in abstract shots, the patterns that lay on the surface of the screen independent of the replication of depth can hold the attention because organization of shape, form and contrast are basic to the act of perception.

A composition can create interest if it achieves the twin objectives of creating depth and also a front surface two-dimensional pattern. This pattern can be created by strong contrast of tone, shape, colour, or texture which simplifies the image. An easy way of judging this quality of the composition is through half-closed eyes which can reveal the main compositional groupings and reduces the awareness of specific visual elements.

Only the content can determine which pattern can be created by balancing out colour, mass, direction, etc. and which aspect of visual design is to be chosen and subjected to the business of pictorial organization. The function of visual design can be shown only by pointing out the meaning it helps to make visible.

Summary

The aim of a balanced composition is to integrate all the visual factors such as shape, colour and location so that no change seems possible. The image achieves unity as a result of all its essential elements.

An unbalanced composition appears accidental and transitory. There is no organizational pattern and any part of the frame could be masked with no loss of communication. There is insufficient arrangement of shapes to assist in grasping the reason for the image. It is ambiguous and unable to hold any visual attention beyond the initial search for understanding.

Visual attention can always be captured by movement. Movement within the frame usually takes precedence over all other compositional devices in attracting attention.

One of the aims of good composition is to find and emphasize structural patterns that the mind/eye can easily grasp.

6
Light

The key visual element

The most important element in the visual design of film and television images is light. Apart from its fundamental role of illuminating the subject, light determines tonal differences, outline, shape, colour, texture and depth. It can create compositional relationships, provide balance, harmony and contrast. It provides mood, atmosphere and visual continuity. Light is the key visual force and is therefore central to any consideration of visual composition.

It is difficult to discuss and separate out, from the range of influences light has on visual communication, the particular influence it has on composition. This section will concentrate on the effect lighting has on contrast and balance.

Harmony and contrast

The Gestalt theories explain the act of perception as a continuous quest to resolve visual confusions, to reduce visual ambiguities and to rationalize and explain. The theories suggest there is a continuing human drive towards equilibrium – that is towards no visual uncertainties. We are unable to switch-off looking (except by closing our eyes) and therefore there is the constant need to understand what we see. The way we achieve understanding is to group and organize diversity, to simplify complex images into regular patterns and to eliminate, where possible, conflicting readings of an image (Figure 6.1).

But there is an equal and opposite force at work in this disposition towards visual simplicity. As we have seen, continuous perceptual attention requires continuous challenges. Perception requires visual puzzles to unravel and decode. If the challenge is too great, if the viewer is supplied with images which make no sense, like a too difficult crossword puzzle, perceptual attention will be discarded once one or two clues have proved unsolvable. But if there is no

ambiguity in a visual image, no uncertainty in the act of perception, if there is a surfeit of simplicity and symmetry, attention will drift and a visual condition close to sleep will be induced. Attention often requires unbalance, visual shock, stimulation and arresting images.

Although perception seeks visual unity, a detailed visual communication requires contrast to articulate its meaning. Morse code can be understood if the distinction between dot and dash is accentuated. A visual message requires the same accentuation of contrast in order to achieve coherent meaning. Light, by supplying contrast of tones, can remove visual ambiguity in a muddle of competing

Figure 6.2 'Office Party' (1977), Patrick Caulfield.

Although perception seeks visual unity, a detailed visual communication requires contrast to articulate its meaning. A dynamic image sets out a visual conflict or tension and a resolution. There is a strong, underlying triangular shape in this painting which anchors the diversity of competing visual elements.

subjects but the wrong tonal contrast can produce a confused and misleading 'message' – the dots and the dashes come close to the same duration and are misread (Figure 6.2).

Communication

Communication is achieved by contrast. The communication carrier – sound or light provides a message by modulation. There is a need for polarities whether loud or soft, dark or light, dot or dash. Meaning is made clear by comparison.

Light is the perfect medium for modulating contrast. It illuminates the subject and is therefore the carrier of the message. Lighting technique, as applied in film and television production, balances out and reduces the contrast ratio to fit the inherent limitations of the medium. It therefore contributes in the drive towards perceptual equilibrium by creating simplified images. But light is also needed to provide modelling, contrast and tonal differences. In this sense it introduces diversity and contrast whilst identifying meaning.

These two competing systems – *harmony*, which tends to balance out conflict of mass and *contrast*, which stresses differences and therefore makes meaning clear – are referred to in Gestalt terminology as tendencies towards levelling and sharpening.

Levelling is the weakening or toning down of irregularity. It is epitomized by the perfect distribution of ratio and balance accomplished in classical art. There are no visual ambiguities or uncertainties of what is displayed either in the objectives of the visual designer or in the perception of the viewer. It is a foolproof visual solution for the inexperienced eye as the rules are self-evidently displayed as ratio, balance and symmetry. But perceptual attention demands stimulation whereas harmony tends towards the elimination of visual conflict. There is a visual design need to introduce tension through contrast.

Sharpening allows clarity of communication through contrast. In its most extreme form the middle tones are eliminated to provide a simplification of the image to the bare essentials (such as Rembrandt displayed in some of his paintings). If the main purpose of a visual statement is to convey ideas, information and feeling, then contrast is required to articulate the image and to focus on the meaning of the message.

A dynamic image is one where a visual conflict or tension has been set up and then resolved. The ying/yang of visual design is harmony and contrast. Harmony, appeases the perceptual system and therefore facilitates the delivery of the message. Contrast grabs the attention and ensures the perceptual system stays switched on to receive the message.

Hard and soft

Within a broad generalization, two qualities of light that are used in film and television production – hard and soft – have a similarity with the sharpening and levelling of the Gestalt terminology.

Usually hard light produces the greatest contrast, modelling and texture. It creates depth, shape and relationships. All light, hard or soft can reveal modelling, texture, contrast – it is a matter of shadow structure which determines the 'sharpness' of the effects. Diffused light is often applied to reduce the contrast introduced by a hard light source and to create an integrated harmony of tones.

Lighting and visual communication

Contrast makes meaning clear. Generally lighting for contrast involves using hard light sources which are often easier to control than a diffuse source. This enables light to be directed and controlled to provide light exactly where it is required and to keep light away from where it is not required. An image with strong contrasts which only emphasizes the required visual elements may appear mannered and artificial because in everyday situations, subjects are not lit in such a precise and controlled way.

Naturally occurring light sources do not discriminate between important and unimportant visual elements ascribed to them by individuals. It is the human mind in the act of perception that attaches relevance to one image as opposed to another. The quest by some lighting designers to replicate naturally occurring lighting effects is at odds with most visual communication such as scripted drama, information, etc., which aims, by selective production techniques, to focus on one aspect in order to communicate a specific message. 'Realistic' lighting (i.e. everyday random and haphazard illumination) will require modification not only to conform to the technical requirements of the medium (e.g. contrast range, minimum exposure, etc.) but also as part of the overall production strategy to be selective in the message produced.

Film and television production is selective in order to communicate. Naturally occurring light illuminates impartially every surface within its orbit making no judgements and exercising no discretion. This is the visual equivalent of the image produced from an unmanned, static security camera.

Controlled lighting and composition

One of the main values of light in relation to composition is the ability to accentuate tonal differences and provide balance or visual unity. Compositional design using light sources relies on control of light direction. Keeping light off surfaces in the field of view can be as important for the composition of the shot as controlling where the light will fall.

Modulating the light pattern of a shot is introducing selective contrast and this is best achieved by a hard light source. But the degree and extent of the artificial contrast or range of tonal values in an image that is introduced by the selective positioning of lamps gives rise to arguments about styles of lighting.

'Realistic' lighting aims to replicate naturally occurring light sources whether sunlight or light naturally found in interiors or exteriors. As an objective, it is nearly always compromised because of the technical considerations of the recording medium. Intercutting between a subject in full frontal sunlight facing a subject who has only naturally occurring reflected light will produce an obvious mismatch. Nearly all subjects illuminated by naturally occurring light sources will need some lighting modification even if it is simply restaging their positions to reduce the worst excesses of uncontrolled light.

Diffused light technique was used in a move away from what many saw as the 'unrealistic' contrast introduced by hard light sources. These selectively lit aspects of a subject and setting especially in what was considered the artificial and mannered three-point portrait lighting system where every face had a key, fill and backlight. Diffused light often eliminates strong modelling and the separation of planes which indicate depth. It may be difficult to separate foreground/ background without some form of backlight or hard light emphasis on selective areas of the frame and therefore the illusion of depth is diminished. The direction and selective coverage of soft light is more difficult to control and therefore inevitably there is less control of tone and mass in a composition. As we have discussed earlier, strong contrast can emphasize meaning and provide attention grabbing dynamic images but at the cost of appearing mannered, artificial or in a word – unrealistic. In normal everyday perception we seldom encounter strong, unequivocal visual statements but neither do we view the world within a frame, without normal binocular depth perception and being subjected to rapid changes of image size. Any two dimensional depiction of reality begins with selection and the drive towards lighting 'realism' is only partly modifying the inherently artificial representation of a television or film image.

Narrative film style

A style of lighting has therefore been developed over many decades which lights the subject in sympathy with the demands of the script.

Figure 6.3 The aim of the lighting cameraman in the golden age of Hollywood Studio production was to make the artiste as handsome or as glamorous as possible.

The resulting image may be at odds with the perceived lighting realism of the setting (e.g. a window as the only source and direction of light may be ignored in a close-up) but is sufficiently 'natural' to be accepted in a flow of images. One of the main influences on this style of lighting was the commercial pressure to exploit the glamour of the leading players.

The domination of the star actor/actress in Hollywood feature film production created a vocabulary of close-ups (CUs), medium close-ups (MCUs), and over-the-shoulder (O/S) shots to emphasize the star. The aim of the lighting cameraman was to make the artiste as handsome or as glamorous as possible. If you could photograph a star well, then the star would get you under contract to the studio they were with (Figure 6.3). The following quotes from cameramen indicate the influence lighting decisions could have – Cameraman Lee Garnes: 'If the scene average light level was 100 ft candles then Dietrich would be lit with 110 ft candles so that her face was the significant part of the frame.' Charles Lang: 'I had to use a high key light to narrow Dietrich's cheek bones. Claudette Colbert could only be shot one side and therefore sets had to be designed for the action to keep that side of face to camera.'

The creation of the studio look in the 1930s was achieved by a strong apprenticeship of assistant cameramen following a specific studio style. Technicians worked on whatever they were allocated to but the studio system allowed them to work on many films and they therefore developed a range of techniques across a diversity of narrative styles. Major studios tended to be known for specific genre films and the look of their films followed the subject. MGM built a reputation for 'glamour', Paramount for 'gloss', Warners for 'hard edge' gritty realism.

Multi-camera television broadcast production followed the same 'industrial' pattern with television technicians allocated to work on a broad range of programmes and techniques ranging from 'Play of the Month' to 'Playschool'. Although there was some specialism, most camera crews and lighting directors were expected to have the techniques required to embrace all the different television programme formats.

The fashion for high contrast, dynamic graphic images reached its apogee in the *Film Noir* style of the 1940s and 1950s which had been heavily influenced by the earlier German expressionist cinema (Figure 6.4). This style of lighting with hard edge shadows and strong contrast has a powerful influence on the composition of the shot. Woody Bredell who photographed 'The Killers' (1946) suggested that the film was lit in order to reduce the detail in the images to the very basic visual information for story telling. This was achieved by strong, single source lighting, by slashes of light, low angles and dark shadows to produce stark imagery.

Figure 6.4 John Alton, the master of **Film Noir** lighting, used strong, single source, slashes of light, low angles and 'unfilled' shadows.

An important function of a hard light source is to provide shadow as well as a lit surface. Deep shadows give an image visual weight. The cameraman John Alton was widely regarded as the definitive exponent of this style of lighting. He was described as 'not being afraid of the dark' and for him, black was the most important element in the shot. He suggested that the most influential lights were the ones he did not turn on. High contrast – deep blacks and highlights – strengthen the core meaning of an image. There is no uncertainty of the principal subject. Figure and ground cannot be mistaken. But strong contrast can tip over into a crude unappealing simplicity which runs out of interest once the initial impact has been absorbed. If the predominant tones of an image are dark and without highlights, the image can convey mystery and suspense and, as used in some television soaps, a form of ersatz realism by avoiding any visual indication that is out of keeping with the setting (e.g. bright highlights on hair provided by backlight). But a surfeit of low key realism can also induce a visual sense of depression leading to indifference.

The *Film Noir* period ended with 'A Touch of Evil' (1958). It was shot by Russell Metty with extraordinary baroque touches made at the same time as the New Wave was emerging in Paris. 'Touch of Evil' anticipated the fluid use of a hand-held camera when Welles had an Eclair Camiflex lightweight European camera imported and it was hand held to great effect in the high contrast interior lit by an external flashing neon sign when the Welles' character murders a small town criminal.

This graphic, hard edged, high contrast lighting style controlled the composition of the shot. Shadow can be used as mass in a framing to balance out other visual elements. The edges between shadow and lit areas can be used in the same way as line convergence is used to focus attention, create depth or to unite foreground and background.

Naturalism

In a more subtle but no less influential way, the use of light by its direction, coverage and intensity can be used for pictorial unity and subject emphasis as an invisible technique. Invisible in the sense that although the lighting direction, intensity and coverage may change between long shot and close up, the lighting design has skilfully disguised the changes to maximize the strength of each image.

In long shot, the lighting emphasis may be on the atmosphere of the room and the subject's relationship with the interior. The lighting will help to integrate the composition of figure and background. In close shot, the lighting may emphasize features of the face and separate subject foreground from background. Broken shadow design on the background may be quite different in pattern between long shot and close shot in order to accommodate the competing emphasis in the individual shots but visual unity is sustained by other lighting controls.

The lighting effect suggested in each shot may match normal experience but if carefully analysed, could not be achieved in that specific situation. The skill of this lighting treatment is to convince and persuade the viewer of the naturalness of the artifice.

Single shot, single camera technique allows the luxury of tailoring composition, lighting and staging to maximize the objective of each shot provided lighting and other visual continuity detail appears consistent. An audience can be convinced of time continuity without an exact match of every visual element carrying over between each shot. A magician who suddenly waves a flag with his left hand while his right hand deftly secretes a prop for his next trick will know that most if not all of his audience will be watching the flag due to his misdirection of their attention. A disguised lighting technique allows each shot to be lit to maximize communication and audience attention.

Continuous multi-camera shooting records an exact visual match between shots. Body position, lighting and setting carry over automatically between shots and therefore often necessitates considerable compromise between the ideal composition and what is available by shooting in real time. It does have the advantage of continuity of performance by the actors/presenters and allows the tempo and interpretation to unravel/unfold over time without the interruption for new set-ups.

The three functions of lighting – illumination, interpretation and medium requirements, all have a bearing on composition. High contrast may provide punchy dynamic images but all productions do not require to communicate with the dramatic intensity of Hamlet. Form follows function in lighting as it does in other creative activities.

In 1855, as the arguments raged about the quest for perfect mechanical reproduction, a photographer Eugene Durieu, rejected the use of light simply as a means of obtaining an exposure rather than as a means of expression and bringing life, mood and modelling to an image. He rejected the mechanistic view of image reproduction and suggested that 'Imitation is neither the means not the aim of art'. The photographer should choose a viewpoint, concentrate interest on the principal subject, control the distribution of light and be as selective as an artist. The argument has continued ever since with the 'realists' attempting to close the gap between audience and action by allowing them to identify and become part of the action (e.g. 'Coronation Street'; 'Eastenders'; 'Brookside', etc.) and the 'expressionists' who hope, by powerful but fantastic imagery, to move, alter or change the audience's attitudes (Bergman, Welles, etc.).

Summary

The most important element in the visual design of film and television images is light. Apart from its fundamental role of illuminating the subject, light determines tonal differences, outline, shape, colour, texture and depth. It can create compositional relationships, provide balance, harmony and contrast. It provides mood, atmosphere and visual continuity. Light is the key visual force and is therefore central to any consideration of visual composition.

Although perception seeks visual unity, a detailed visual communication requires contrast to articulate its meaning. Light, by supplying contrast of tones, can remove visual ambiguity in a muddle of competing subjects.

These two competing systems – *harmony*, which tends to balance out conflict of mass and *contrast*, which stresses differences and therefore makes meaning clear – are referred to in Gestalt terminology as tendencies towards levelling and sharpening.

Levelling is the weakening or toning down of irregularity. It is epitomized by the perfect distribution of ratio and balance as achieved in classical art. But perceptual attention demands stimulation whereas harmony tends towards the decrement of visual conflict. There is a visual design need to introduce tension through contrast.

Sharpening allows clarity of communication through contrast. If the main purpose of a visual statement is to convey ideas, information and feeling then contrast is required to articulate the image and to focus on the meaning of the message.

A dynamic image is one where a visual conflict or tension has been set up and then resolved. The ying/yang of visual design is harmony and contrast. Harmony, appeases the perceptual system and therefore facilitates the delivery of the message. Contrast grabs the attention and ensures the perceptual system stays switched on to receive the message.

Within a broad generalization, two qualities of light that are used in film and television production – hard and soft – have a similarity with the sharpening and levelling of the Gestalt terminology. Hard light produces contrast, modelling and texture. It creates depth, shape and relationships. Diffused light is often applied to reduce the contrast introduced by a hard light source and to create an integrated harmony of tones.

7
Colour

Colour as subject

Twentieth-century painting has often employed colour as the primary means of visual communication. In their relationship within a frame, colours provide their own kind of balance, contrast, rhythm, structure, texture and depth independent of any recognizable figurative subject that may be defined in terms of line or tone. Colour not only has a profound influence on composition, in many forms of image making, it is the *subject* of the composition.

The importance of colour to express emotional states or to create sensations of movement and space has not always been recognized. Up to the early Renaissance period, colour was considered by many art patrons as an embellishment to a painting to be selected from a list of expensive pigments. Colour was added as a beautifying agent and priced accordingly. For many years, painters blocked in the main structure of a painting primarily in line and tone. Colour was used to supplement the linear and tonal expression of ideas. Although painters began to appreciate the expressive use of colour, the scientific investigation into colour theory by Goethe, Helmholtz, Chevreul and others in the nineteenth century provided the stimulus to reinforce or confirm many painter's intuitive understanding of the effects of colour. Eventually, the optical sensations of colour were fascinating enough to be able to provide the very subject matter of a picture.

Monochrome

Both film and TV began as a black and white medium. In fact film began with no colour, no sound and with very little if any camera movement. The ability to record infinite detail mechanically and the novelty of its 'realism' compensated the photographic image for its lack of colour. Television, by adding the ability to witness an event as it occurred, wherever it occurred, could also compensate for the absence of colour.

The legacy of monochrome television

The gradual transition in the 1960s to colour broadcasting and the gradual replacement of black and white receivers with near universal colour reception left behind one legacy of monochrome television. Nearly all broadcast television cameras are fitted, as standard, with monochrome viewfinders. There are exceptions, but the majority of cameras in daily use up to, and including the introduction of high-definition equipment, use monochrome viewfinders to acquire the basic material for colour television.

Camera manufacturers explain this paradox as their inability, so far, to provide a 1.5" monocular colour viewfinder with sufficient resolution added to their claim that the cost of doing so would be prohibitive. Despite the vast technological changes that have occurred with the development of television cameras in the last fifty years, the one consistent technique that has remained unchanged has been the need for cameramen to use a monochrome viewfinder even when composing colour pictures.

Problems associated with monochrome viewfinders

One of the most common misconceptions with this situation is the myth that there is no need for a colour viewfinder except where colour differentiation is necessary, for example sports coverage, snooker, etc. The camera manufacturers believe that the viewfinder is simply there to be used for focus and what they term 'the adjustment of the picture angle'.

The fact that colour plays a significant part in picture composition is either ignored or conveniently becomes the responsibility of other technicians in the television production chain. After thirty years of transition from monochrome to colour, cameramen remain the last group of black-and-white viewers.

The result of framing up a composition in monochrome often results in the over-reliance on tone, mass and linear design as the main ingredient of the composition. If a colour monitor is accessible, then adjustment can be made for the colour component of the shot but only too often, the frame of reference for the composition is the monochrome viewfinder or a small portable low quality colour monitor. Colours of similar brightness such as red and the darker shades of green merge and may be indistinguishable in the monochrome viewfinder and yet, as separate hues, they exercise a strong influence on the composition. Saturated red and blue appear much darker in a monochrome viewfinder than their brightness value in colour. A small saturated colour against a complementary background has a much greater impact in colour than its viewfinder reproduction (Figure 7.1).

To some extent monochrome pictures are more abstract than colour and the effect of the image is different from our normal colour perception. The image can be more streamlined if only tone and line are considered as compositional elements. Film cameramen after years of black-and-white photography had difficulty in adjusting to

Figure 7.1 Framing up on a 'red' flower which is easily identified by eye against the fence but is difficult to see in monochrome. Composition in monochrome is usually based on mass, line and tone.

the complexity of colour composition compared to the simplicity and control of monochrome. Many photographers still prefer to avoid colour in order to emphasize the form and shape of an image.

It is possible to demonstrate that a video image has been composed in monochrome by switching out the colour on the receiver. It is surprising how much strength is re-introduced into a shot which was originally composed in black and white when the colour content is removed. The reverse can also be seen when a shot could have been improved if a colour viewfinder had been available in order to actively use colour in the composition in addition to line and tone.

A flat lit scene viewed in black and white gives the impression of lack of contrast and punch whereas the same scene in colour may be much more acceptable than the monochrome rendering suggests. A shot lit with predominantly red light has very little contrast and low modulation when viewed through a monochrome viewfinder. This often provokes an unnecessary struggle by the cameraman using a monochrome viewfinder to provide dynamic compositions using mass and line which is quite unnecessary when the same shot is viewed in colour.

Contrast lighting may provide compositions with mor
whereas overcast light may give flat black-and-white p
although the colour content may help to separate subject matt
In a monochrome viewfinder, the lack of contrast dilutes the visu
strength and without strong light/dark relationships the composition
may often appear to be lacking balance or emphasis. If reliance is
placed on monochrome viewfinder compositions, some colour
combinations may have a striking dissimilarity to the balanced black-
and-white compatible image.

Composing with a monochrome viewfinder results in emphasizing
contrast, mass and usually the convergence of lines. Colour becomes
simply the accidental effect of individual objects within the frame
rather than the conscious grouping and locating of colour within the
frame. The weight of colour elements are not used to balance the
composition and can frequently unbalance the considered monochrome composition of tone and line.

The nature of colour

Human perception compensates for changes in colour whereas the
correctly set-up video camera records colour as it is and not as we
perceive it. The cameraman therefore has to concern himself with
the accuracy of the recorded colour. He must be aware of the
changes in colour temperature and balance the camera to compensate unless a specific colour cast is required. He must be aware of
reflected or direct coloured light from outside the frame that illuminates or degrades the subject of the shot.

Colour and Composition

The relative quality of colour

The faithful reproduction of colour requires techniques to ensure
that the specific colours of a scene are reproduced accurately and
colour continuity requires that the same colours are identically
reproduced in succeeding shots. This is often a basic requirement in
most types of camerawork but colour as an emotional influence in
establishing atmosphere or in structuring a composition, also plays a
vital role in visual communication.

Terms used to describe colour can sometimes lead to confusion.
In this account hue refers to the quality which distinguishes one
colour from another (e.g. blue, red, green, etc.). Brightness is the
tonal quality of a colour – its relative brightness in relation to other
colours (i.e. brightness is a perceived comparison not a measurement
of a specific tone) and chroma refers to the quality of saturation of
the specific colour.

The perception of the apparent hue of any coloured object is likely
to vary depending on the colour of its background and the colour
temperature of the light illuminating it. Staging someone in a yellow
jacket against green foliage will produce a different contrast relationship to staging the same person against a blue sky.

There appears to be a reduction in the perception of 'colourful-ness' under a dull overcast sky. The muted affect on colour under diffused light can often allow colours to blend and provide a softer pastel relationship and a satisfactory picture whereas the lack of contrast may produce flat, drab monochrome images.

Sunlight raises the general level of illumination and provides a directional light which, reflected off coloured objects, tends to increase the 'colourfulness' of a scene compared to the diffuse light of an overcast sky. A proportion of directional light is reflected as white specular from glossy surfaces and increases the impact of colour. The hard modelling and greater contrast make the scene look more 'alive'.

The perceptual impact of a coloured object is not consistent but is modified by the quality of the light illuminating it, by reflection, shadow and by its relationship with surrounding colours.

Balancing a composition with colour

Balance in a composition depends on the distribution of visual weight. Mass, relative brightness, line and the psychological impor-tance of a visual element can all be structured to provide visual unity in an image and to provide a route for the eye to travel in order to emphasize the most important element. Colour can be used to balance and to unify an image in many ways.

An out-of-focus single hued object within the frame (e.g. red), often exerts a strong influence in the composition and may distract attention from the main subject.

Light/dark relationships

As we have seen, the eye is attracted to the lightest part of an image or that part of the image which has the greatest contrast and if colour is reproduced as a grey scale, yellow, after white, is the brightest colour. Depending on their backgrounds, a small area of yellow for example, will carry more visual weight than a small area of blue. When balancing out a composition attention should be paid to the relative brightness of colour and its location within the frame.

Cold/warm contrast

Many colours have a hot or a cold feel to them. Red is considered hot and blue is thought of as cold. People disagree about how hot or how cold a particular colour may be but the general perceptual consensus is that hot colours advance and cold colours recede. This has a compo-sitional significance of colour as a depth indicator and affects the control of the principal subject. It will take other strong design elements within a shot to force a foreground blue object to exist in space in front of a red object. The eye naturally sees red as closer than blue unless the brightness, shape, chroma value and background of the blue is so arranged that in context it becomes more dominant than the desaturated, low brightness of the red. Colour effects are relative and no one set of guidelines will hold true for all colour relationships. For example, the intensity of a hot colour can be emphasized by surround-ing it by cool colours. The intensity of the contrast will affect balance and to what part of the frame the eye is attracted.

Complementary contrast

Painters have long been aware that balance can be achieved by opposing a colour with its complementary. They have used green as the complementary of red; blue as the complementary of orange; and yellow as the complementary of violet. These complementary pairings consist of a hot and a cold colour. Complementaries placed alongside each other will appear to have more vividness and vitality than colours that are adjacent in the colour wheel.

Visual equilibrium, however, is not simply achieved by equal areas of complementary pairs. Blue needs a greater area to balance its complementary orange. Red needs approximately the same area of green whereas yellow needs a relatively small area of violet to achieve visual equilibrium.

Red and green primary colours have different brightness values when depicted on a monochrome viewfinder. When judging balance in a composition using a monochrome viewfinder it is therefore easy to mistakenly provide a larger area of the lighter tone green to balance out the weight of the darker tone red. This will produce an unbalanced colour image.

Area of colour

The balancing of area and the shape of a coloured object has a strong impact on the unity of an image. A small area of intense colour can unbalance a composition and continually attract the eye. If its location coincides with the main subject of the shot then the right emphasis is achieved. If it exists near the edge of frame or away from the dominant subject then it acts as a second subject of interest and is a distraction.

Individual experience of colour

Colour perception is often associated with feeling and it has been suggested that whereas colour produces an emotional experience, the response to shape corresponds to intellectual control.

The individual response to colour may be a product of fashion and culture – a learnt relationship, or it may be an intrinsic part of the act of perception. People's colour preferences have been tested and in general western people choose, in order of preference, blue, red, green, purple, orange, yellow. This choice is modified when the colour is associated with an object that has a specific use. For example, the majority preference expressed for a range of colours for cars are different from the majority choice for a range of acceptable colours for toothbrushes. Colour preference for dress, decoration and consumer products, etc., is influenced by fashion, social attitudes and temperament.

Colour association

Colour can communicate experience or feeling by association. Red is often described as passionate, stimulating and exciting. Blue is seen as sad and depressing. Yellow is serene or gay whilst green is thought of as restful and stable.

Strong prolonged stimulation of one colour has the effect of decreasing the sensitivity to that colour but sensitivity to its complementary is enhanced. Looking at a saturated red for example for some time and then shifting the gaze to a grey area will provoke a sensation of blue-green. This effect of successive contrast is a result of a process of adaption by the cones and rods in the eye. Intercutting with shots containing strong saturated primaries may give rise to 'after' images of complementary colours.

Colour symbolism

There have been a number of theories based on general colour association concerning the symbolism of colour. Hollywood cameraman Villorio Storaro used his own colour theory in shooting 'The Lost Emperor' where he equated different colours with different moods or atmospheres. The shots at the beginning of the Forbidden City and the family were predominantly orange. He used yellow for personal growth of the young emperor and the realization of personal identity. Yellow was also the royal colour of the Chinese. Yellow dissolved to green with the arrival of the tutor – the arrival of knowledge.

Nestor Almendros used the 'magic hour', that moment of the day when the sun has left the sky and the earth and the sky are bathed in a golden light. There were barely 25 minutes each day of this quality of light to shoot the film 'Days of Heaven' (1978) but it was considered that the contribution of the emotional quality of the light was worth the extra budget required.

Summary

Balance in a composition depends on the distribution of visual weight. Colour can be used to balance and to unify an image in many ways. If the weight of colour elements is ignored (or unseen), it can frequently unbalance the considered monochrome composition of tone and line. A composition framed in monochrome may result in the over-reliance on tone, mass and linear design as the main ingredient of the composition. Colour not only has a profound influence on composition, in many forms of image making, it is the *subject* of the composition.

The perceptual impact of a coloured object is not consistent but is modified by the quality of the light illuminating it, by reflection, shadow and by its relationship with surrounding colours. The individual response to colour may be a product of fashion and culture – a learnt relationship, or it may be an intrinsic part of the act of perception.

8
Past influences

Intuition

Many cameramen insist that composition is intuitive and assume that framing decisions are based on personal and subjective opinion. Even a cursory examination of an evening's output of television will demonstrate the near uniformity of standard conventions in composition. The exceptions to what is considered 'good' composition are either provided by inexperienced cameramen who have yet to become aware of professional techniques (e.g. 'video diaries') or those productions where there has been a conscious decision to be 'different'. This usually entails misframing conventional shots in the mistaken belief that something new and original has been created. In effect, it is simply mispronouncing standard visual language.

These conventions are learnt and do not arise spontaneously as intuitive promptings. Their origins are to be found in changes in painting styles over the last five hundred years, in the influence of still photography and in changes in the style and the technology of film and television production.

No one working in the media can escape the influence of past solutions to visual problems. The evidence is contained in the products of nearly a century of film making and half a century of television production. These are consciously or unconsciously absorbed from the moment we begin to watch moving images. Whereas most people never concern themselves with the nature of these influences, anyone who wishes to make a career in visual communication should be aware of the changes and influences on current conventions in composition and examine the assumptions that may underpin their own 'intuitive' practices.

Early influences

Greek and Renaissance ideals

The concept of proportion and ratio in composition played an important part in Greek/Roman art and architecture and reappears in

Figure 8.1 To create a 'Golden Rectangle', use the diagonal of one half of a square (a) as a radius to extend the dimensions of the square. The 'Golden Rectangle' has the proportions a:b = c:a and was extensively used by the Greeks in architectural design and by Renaissance painters and architects.

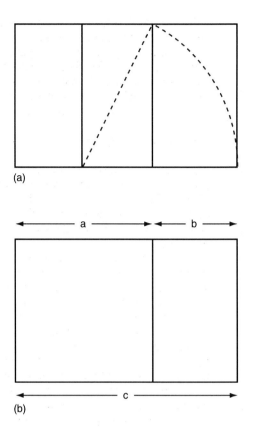

(a)

(b)

some contemporary discussion in the 'format' war (see Chapter 4, Aspect ratio).

The ratio of the longest side of a rectangle to the shortest side is called the aspect ratio of the image. In television for many years this was 4:3, close to the Academy ratio for cinema feature films. Cinemascope ratio of 2.35:1 is now joined by the widescreen format 16:9 and there is even a proposal from the American Society of Cinematographers that a more pleasing format would be a 2:1 ratio (see Figure 4.5).

The ancient Greeks were also interested in the ideal proportions of rectangles and discovered that a ratio, where the value of the longest side divided by the shortest side equalled 1.618, had remarkable arithmetical, algebraical and geometrical properties. Renaissance scholars and painters rediscovered this ratio and Leonardo dubbed it 'The Divine Proportion'. It subsequently became known as the Golden Section. The television widescreen ratio of 16:9 comes close to this preferred ratio.

Compositional balance using this ratio revolves around positioning the main visual elements on the subdivisions obtained by dividing the golden section according to a prescribed formula (Figure 8.1).

Another convention of Renaissance composition especially with religious subjects, is to position the main subject in the centre of the frame and then to balance this with equal weight subjects on either side (see Figure 6.1).

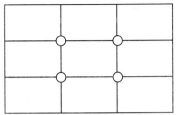

(a) Golden rectangle

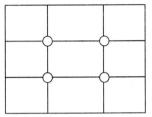

(b) 4 x 3 TV aspect ratio

Figure 8.2 (a) The 'Rule of Thirds' proposes that a useful starting point for any compositional grouping is to place the main subject of interest on any one of the four intersections made by two equally spaced horizontal and vertical lines. Dividing the frame into areas of one-third and two-thirds is a method of constructing a golden rectangle (1.618:1) and these intersections were often used to position key elements of the composition. (b) The standard TV ratio 4x3 (1.33:1) is smaller than this but the Golden Rectangle 'thirds' convention is still applied. Super 16 mm (1.69:1) and Pal Plus widescreen (1.78:1) comes closer to the 1.618:1 of the Golden Rectangle.

The equal duplication of figures on either side of the main subject gives the centre figure importance but splits the composition into two halves and can produce two equally competing subjects of interest. This style of precise formal balance on either side of the frame contrasts with later fashions in composition which sought, by more dynamic visual design, to create a strong sense of movement by leading the eye, by line and structure, around the frame.

The Rule of Thirds

The academic emphasis on proportion and ratio was probably the precursor to a popular compositional convention called the Rule of Thirds. This 'rule' proposes that a useful starting point for any compositional grouping is to place the main subject of interest on any one of the four intersections made by two equally spaced horizontal and vertical lines (Figures 8.2a and 8.2b).

The ratio of dividing the frame into areas of one-third and two-thirds is close to the approximation of a golden section division. These ratios occur so often in western art, architecture and design that they became almost a visual convention. The proportions are learnt and anticipated in a way which is similar to the expectation of a listener to the resolution of musical harmony. Because of this unconscious anticipation, composition based on academic principles can seem stale and static to those people who have experienced the avalanche of visual imagery generated by contemporary technology. A repetitive simple tune can rapidly lose its appeal if continuously heard. Compositions that provide no visual surprises are quickly 'consumed' and require no second appraisal.

The influence of photography

After the invention of the photographic image in the 1830s, the initial novelty of accurate, realistic portraiture gave way to attempts at photographic 'art'. Photographers grouped their subjects according to the academic conventions of the day and were inclined to favour themes and subjects similar to academic painting. The long exposure required by the early photographic process also required the subjects to remain stiff and immobile to avoid blurring. The evolution of faster film allowed snapshot street scenes to be captured. The composition now consisted of enclosing a frame around a continuing event and this resulted, compared to academic painting, in unbalanced and scattered compositional groupings.

People were captured on the move, entering and leaving frame which resulted in quite different images from the carefully posed groups of the long exposure film. The accidental quality of these snapshot compositions were considered by many to be more realistic and life-like than the immobile studio set-ups. Painters were attracted by the sense of movement that could be suggested by allowing subjects to hovver on the edge of the frame (Figure 8.3).

When the frame cuts a figure there is the implication that the frame position is arbitrary, that the scene is endless and a portion of the event just happened to be cut by the frame at that point by chance. The accidental character of the boundary was indeed arbitrary in many snapshots but as a conscious compositional device,

Figure 8.3 'Place de la Concord'
(Vicomete Ludvic Lepic and his
daughters) (1875), Degas.

it had been used centuries before in Donattelo reliefs and in paintings by Mantegna and it is to be found, as a considered design
element, in Japanese painting (Figure 8.4).

In an outside broadcast event the viewer may be aware that they
are being shown selected 'portions' of the event and that the frame
can be instantly adjusted by zooming in, to provide more detailed
information or by zooming out, to include more of the televised event.

Photography developed a compositional style of the instantaneous
framing of an everyday event. The most effective 'freeze frame'
images of arrested motion use the tension created by subjects moving
apart from each other, and the relationship of subjects (often on the
edge of frame) in opposition to their environment. The considered
'spontaneity' of advertising imagery is an artifice carefully crafted to
make use of naturally occurring events and presented in an attempt
at innocent simplicity and naturalness. The sophisticated technique
used to create a seemingly accidental, non-designed image is a long
way removed from the typical 'holiday' snapshotter who haphazardly
puts a frame around an event and rarely achieves a print with the
impact of the controlled image made by an experienced photographer. The quality of 'random chance' in a composition therefore
contains many formal devices which an experienced photographer
will employ and exploit.

In copying from photographs in the mid-nineteenth century, artists
attempted to correct this lack of order, the unnaturalness of the
snapshot and the lack of pictorial logic according to academic
compositional principles. The distortion of perspective which
sometimes gives the snapshot its special power and the accidents of

Figure 8.4 'The Haneda Ferry and Benten Shrine' (1858), Hiroshige. This composition pre-dates the widespread use of wide angle foreground framing in film and television.

composition were ironed out when painters translated photographs into paintings. Degas was attracted by the 'snapshot' style from sources which had no recognized style. Degas may have recognized that the 'non-style' of snapshot composition had a vitality lacking in conventional groupings and gave it artistic respectability by using in many of his paintings, the characteristics of the arbitrary frame and perspective of short exposure photography (see Figure 8.3).

More recent influences

If photographic imagery provided an alternative to an over intellectual approach to composition, many late nineteenth-century and early twentieth-century painters also challenged the received conventions of academic subject and design. Part of their traditional role of providing a visual record of faces and places was also being eroded by the growth of photography.

The predominant style of painting in the mid-nineteenth century favoured realistic illusionism. Photography in providing an accurate imitation of external realities reinforced this existing fashion and to some extent supplanted the social role of the artist as the only supplier of visual copies of nature, people or places.

In the 1840s, photographic portraiture challenged the traditional painted portrait. This was followed in the 1850s, as the emerging technology allowed, by a fashion for landscape photography. Increasing film sensitivity during the next three decades permitted shutter speeds of up to 1/1000th second to be used and enabled fast moving objects to be frozen. Artists discovered that their customary way of depicting objects in motion were false even though they appeared to correspond to normal perception.

The increased shutter speeds of the 1860s and 1870s allowed snapshot compositions of normal everyday street activity, subjects which had rarely been thought suitable for painting. This type of urban realism not only displayed a new type of composition, utilizing the accidental and random design of people and traffic, frozen in motion, but also provided new viewpoints of these events such as the high angle shot from the top of a building looking down on to a street. When, in the late 1880s, Kodak announced 'You press the button – we do the rest', a flood of new 'image makers' were unleashed, unfettered by academic art training or academic precepts.

Realism was considered by some to be the new enemy of art and it was thought to have been nurtured by the growth of photography. Those artists who considered photographs to be no more than 'reflections in a looking glass', had to consider what personal aesthetic qualities they brought to their own paintings. In many cases they moved away from an attempt at the literal imitation of nature to more impressionistic images and later, to colour and form as the prime subject of their work. If the camera alone was to be the final arbiter in questions concerning visual truths then artists would move to new themes and subjects and explore the underlying structure of the psychology of perception and the ambiguity of imagery. They explored the differences between what one saw and what one knew about the subject.

Apart from the early photographic attempts to mimic academic painting subjects and groupings, the influence in the nineteenth century appeared to flow from photographs to painting. When painting found new themes and forms away from realistic illusionism in the twentieth century, photographers followed their lead and also attempted to place more emphasis on form and structure – on the abstraction of design from nature.

The use of simple shapes devoid of detail, patterns produced by everyday objects, the reduction of tone, colour producing sharp contrasts, 'distressed' texture and fragments of printed ephemera are popular photographic images influenced by the changing styles in painting in the first decades of the twentieth century.

There developed a two-way influence between painting and photography with some artists rejecting the Renaissance perspective of a single viewpoint and ultimately eliminating figurative subjects from their frame. Many became interested in creating compositions of colour, line and tone abstracted from three-dimensional objects.

These investigations into the nature of two-dimensional pattern on a surface influenced photographers who used monochrome to simplify the image and to create semi-abstract designs of line, light and shade. Many contemporary photographic images used in advertising are influenced by the experiments carried out in painting seventy or eighty years ago.

A painter has control of all the design elements in his painting and works towards a particular effect. A photographer, recognizing the freshness of the design, can find a parallel image and by careful selection recreate the more abstract graphic image of fine art. The cycle of 'new' art image followed by repetition and recreation within photography (particularly in advertising) all occurred during the twentieth century. The process reached a peak in the 1960s when painting incorporated advertising imagery. This reworking of the original commercial graphic conventions was immediately reclaimed by advertising and emerged as a new photographic style.

Photographic style

There was anxiety in the mid 1860s of the growing photographic style in painting. There was fierce resistance from the academic exhibitions to hanging paintings which appeared to be based on photographs and there was a heated debate about the nature of photographic style.

As we have discussed, one aspect of monochrome compositions is the tendency to emphasize line and tone. Also, people were unused to some types of photographic perspective which, although often identical to retina perspective, remained ignored or unacknowledged due to size constancy (see Chapter 3, Perspective). Photographic perspective, conditioned by size of reproduction, lens position, distance from subject and focal length, appeared to many people to be unnatural and distorted compared to perspective used in painting. Usually it was 'unpainterly' subjects which emphasized what was considered perspective distortions.

Photography allowed the most accurate reproduction of the most minute detail which incited great interest in the general public even though as one artist claimed, there is no great visual truth in counting how many slates there are on an image of a roof.

Although the eye unconsciously changes focus depending on the distance of the subject of interest, the degree of 'out of focus' of subjects at other distances goes unrecognized. Depending on the aperture used, a camera's depth-of-focus produces an image which may blur the foreground and background of a subject. This photographic zone of focus effect created a new visual representation of depth.

Alternative viewpoints, such as a high angle from a building looking down on to a street, appeared to be a photographic innovation unseen in painting. The ability, with high shutter speeds and extreme magnification, to reveal visual truths unavailable to normal human perception were amongst other photographic innovations that excited interest. Even blurred motion and photographic defects such as halation provided inspiration for artists such as Corot to experiment with new painting conventions.

The creation of 'invisible' technique

The ability to record an event on film was achieved in the latter part of the nineteenth century. During the next two decades, there was the transition from the practice of running the camera continuously to record an event, to the stop/start technique of separate shots where the camera was repositioned between each shot in order to film new material. The genesis of film narrative was established.

At first, audiences were amazed just to see moving pictures. A shot of a train bearing down on them from the screen appeared so lifelike that some people screamed with fright. The novelty of the medium had a powerful impact on audiences and the technique required to sustain that interest needed little more than to point the camera at the event and to keep cranking the handle to wind the complete reel through the camera until the film or the event ended.

The screen was conceived as an acting area similar to the stage as seen by an audience in a theatre. The action moved around the screen space without either the camera moving or the size of shot changing. All the techniques that we are familiar with now had to be learnt in the first two decades of this century. The first film makers had to experiment and invent the grammar of editing, shot size and the variety of camera movements that are now standard.

There was a moment in this development when someone first had the idea of moving the camera closer, or using a closer lens, to provide an image of a person in close up. Someone else had the idea of putting the camera in a car or train and filmed the first tracking shot. As early as 1897, a camera was placed in a gondola and provided camera movement in 'Le Grand Canal à Venice'. The panning shot was invented when someone slowly moved the camera across a landscape or street scene.

As well as camera movement came the problems involved in stopping the camera, moving to a new position and starting the camera again. The ability to find ways of shooting subjects and then editing the shots together without distracting the audience was learnt by the commercial cinema over a number of years.

The guiding concept that connected all these developing techniques of camera movement and shot change was the need to persuade the audience that they were watching continuous action in real time. This required the mechanics of film making to be hidden from the audience – to be invisible.

Standard camerawork conventions

The technique of changing shot without distracting the audience was learnt over a number of years. A number of 'invisible' techniques were discovered and became the standard conventions of film making and later television. These included continuity cutting and parallel action cutting, variation in shot size and not crossing 'the line', matching camera movement to action, lighting for mood, glamour and atmosphere and editing for pace and variety.

Many film techniques evolved from the necessity of stitching together a number of shots filmed out of sequence. The technique needed to persuade the intended audience that they were watching a continuous event. A seamless string of images was designed to hide the methods of film production and to convince the spectator that the fabrication constructed by many weeks of film making had a believable reality. Camera and editing technique contrived to prevent the viewer becoming conscious that they were watching an elaborate replica. The means by which the counterfeit was constructed had to be hidden in order to persuade and therefore camera technique had to be invisible.

Early film technique had the camera firmly fastened to a tripod although some camera movement was achieved by mounting the camera on a moving vehicle or craft. Panning heads gradually came into use after 1900 and the standard lens appears to have been a 25° or a 17°. Framing was similar to contemporary still photography with staging similar to a theatre presentation.

Reverse angles, point of view shots and position matching on cuts were all discovered and became standard technique. The evolution of the grammar of film technique was not instantaneous or self-evident. Each visual technique, such as parallel tracking with the action, had to be invented, refined and accepted by other film makers before entering the repertoire of standard camera practice.

The thread that linked most of these developments was the need to provide a variety of ways of presenting visual information coupled with the need for them to be unobtrusive in their transition from shot to shot. Expertly used, they were invisible and yet provided the narrative with pace, excitement and variety. These criteria are still valid and much of the pioneering work in the first decades of the century remains intact in current camera technique.

Lens-angle and camera position

Distinctive compositions which only made sense in the context of the film narrative (such as point-of-view shots) occurred pre-1914 when high and low angles began to be used. This style of composition, although not unique to film, was infrequently used in the still photography of the day.

Another convention which had an important influence on the composition of the shot was known as the 'Vitagraph Angle'. The Vitagraph Studio from about 1909 used a line perpendicular to the camera drawn nine feet from the lens as an indicator of the nearest point the actor could approach the camera. The lens was positioned at chest height as opposed to the common practice of eye height and this produced foreground heads of figures higher in the frame than background figures. It also produced a closer shot than the current staging of actors to no more than twelve foot from the camera resulting in full-length figures. At times the camera was positioned at waist height which resulted in a more dynamic relationship between foreground and background. These departures from head high lens position also eliminated the large amount of dead space above the actors' heads seen in many films of the period.

Multi-camera live television conventions

Film is a record of an event edited and assembled after the event occurs. Live television is a presentation of an event as it occurs. The unique quality of an electronic camera is its ability to produce a picture that can be instantly transmitted. This entails a production technique which involves a number of people perfecting their individual contribution in a production group simultaneously as the event is transmitted. To co-ordinate such a group activity, it is essential to plan and have some measure of rehearsal before transmission or to rely on standard production conventions which are understood by everyone involved.

Standard television multi-camera conventions grew out of film technique and the same objective of disguising technique in order to suspend disbelief in the viewer was adopted. The problem for actuality television was not to recreate 'real time' as in discontinuous film shooting but to meld together multi-camera shooting of an actuality event so that, for example, change of camera angle or cutting between different shot sizes was not obtrusive and distracting to the viewer. The aim once again was towards an 'invisible technique'.

As multi-camera television camerawork dealt with uninterrupted action in a time scale created by the nature of the event covered, 'real' time had to be continuously covered in a mixture of shot sizes and or camera development. Shot size became standardized around abbreviated shot descriptions such as MCU (medium close up), CU (close-up), MS (medium shot), LS (long shot) and o/s 2s (over-the-shoulder two-shot), etc., in order that matched shot size could be achieved to allow invisible cuts between cameras. Cameramen had to provide cutting points either pre-rehearsed or by monitoring what the rest of the camera crew were providing. Same size shots of the same subject would not cut together neither would widely different amounts of head room. Idiosyncratic personal composition by a cameraman would remain unnoticed if they were responsible for the whole of the visual production but would immediately be apparent if intercut with standard camera technique provided by the rest of the crew. Camera technique remained invisible provided it conformed to certain criteria. These conventions are inherited by everyone working within live or multi-camera recordings unless there is a production requirement for shot change to be obtrusive and obvious.

How the introduction of the zoom affected television picture composition

Before the introduction of colour television in the late 1960s, most television productions were shot using prime lenses. Although zooms were extensively used on outside broadcasts, many studio productions used cameras which were fitted with a rotating turret equipped with four lenses of different focal length. The precise lens-angle depended on tube size and camera manufacturers but the four standard focal lengths chosen had lens-angles of approximately 35°, 24°, 16° and 8°.

Because of the standardization of lens-angle, camera scripts and studio floor plans were produced giving the lens-angle and camera position for each shot. Although shots were modified during rehearsal, the initial choice of lens influenced the look of the production and established a discipline of matched size and perspective of intercut shots. Over time, each prime lens was recognized to have a well-defined role in multi-camera studio production.

The 24° was considered the 'natural' perspective lens and allowed camera movement and was often used on 'two' shots or 'three' shots. The 16° and the 8° were close-up lenses and although an occasional camera movement was attempted on the 16°, it was likely to result in an unsteady frame due to tracking over an uneven studio floor and the difficulty of holding frame with a fluid head using a narrow angle. Camera movement with an 8° lens intensified this problem and was seldom if ever used for tracking.

Narrow depth of field also inhibited camera movement on these lenses as the cameraman had to physically move the camera himself, adjust the framing and follow focus. This required three hands if constant focus pulls were required on the narrow lens.

The 35° lens was considered 'wide angle' and allowed complex shot development without the twin problems of focus and the considerable amount of camera movement required to achieve significant change of viewpoint if a smaller lens-angle was employed. (see Chapter 10, Movement, for discussion on the different arcs of movement required for different lens-angles).

This arrangement of a set of four lenses created a tight discipline in production and aided the twin objectives of matched shot size and perspective matching. Two cameras being intercut on two people talking would, as a matter of good technique, use the same lens-angle and camera position/height relative to the participants. The introduction of colour cameras which were universally fitted with a zoom due to the need for precise alignment of the lens to the four and later three tubes required for colour, caused a significant change in picture composition and in camera movement.

In the first years of television colour production, there was a determined effort to continue with the four-lens convention by using a zoom shot box which had been pre-set to the four standard lens-angles. Tracking the camera was usually favoured in preference to zooming although pop music programmes quickly utilized the visual impact of zooming.

As the range of zoom angles increased, a greater variety of shot sizes were possible from any specific camera position. This allowed the perspective of some types of conventional shots to change considerably. Zoom lenses with a 55° wide angle became common and allowed a shot development which was more dynamic due to the greater exaggeration of artist to background movement. At the narrow end of the zoom, lens-angles of 5° allowed close-ups of artistes at the back of the set with the corresponding reduction in the perspective of the depth of the shot.

The most noticeable change in the style of television camerawork came with the use of the zoom to accommodate movement, to trim the shot depending on the action. Whereas in the past, with monochrome cameras, the staging of the artistes may have been re-positioned during the blocking of the show to accommodate a fixed lens-angle, a flexible lens-angle allowed the shot to be recomposed by zooming in or out. Gradually lens-angle and camera position were not pre-plotted but relied on the flexibility of the zoom as a variable lens-angle to find acceptable framing. This was sometimes to the detriment of matched shots. Intercut shots could be matched on size if not on lens perspective by a rapid adjustment of the zoom. The prejudice against zooming even in drama was relaxed until a point was reached where zooming predominated in television production.

The compositional distinction between zoom and track

One of the characteristics of camera movement as compared to zooming is that it approximates to human perception which experiences changes in size relationships as the physical position of the viewpoint alters. Tracking into a scene will alter the size relationship of background to foreground objects as they flow past the lens. In this sense it can be claimed that tracking is more 'realistic' than zooming.

Tracking into a scene extends the involvement of the viewer in that they are being allowed visually to move into the two-dimensional screen space. In normal perception, depth indicators can be appraised or checked by moving the head or the body to seek a new viewpoint of the field of view. Viewing a series of static images on a two-dimensional screen does not allow this visual 'interrogation'. If depth is to be indicated it must be self-evident and contained in the composition of the image. A tracking shot provides a change in viewpoint and allows the viewer greater opportunity to experience the depth of the space pictured compared to either a zoom or a static shot.

A zoom in or out contains no change in size relationships, it simply allows either a greater magnification of a portion of the shot or a wider view of the same size relationships. The arguments for zooming (apart from convenience and budget) is that as a film or television production is a highly artificial process, the viewer is already experiencing a radically different visual sensation watching a two-dimensional image of an object (which is either magnified or extremely diminished) compared to their visual experience when observing the actual event. If so much is changed in the translation by the film and television medium using techniques of shot size, perspective, two dimensions, small image, etc. why quibble about zooming which fails to reproduce some small physical aspect of human perception.

A film or television production is an approximation of an event which often includes attempts to induce an experience of the event in the viewer. Zooming creates a visual experience and therefore, it is argued, is as valid a technique as any other artifice employed.

Portable cameras

With the widespread use of portable video camera/recorders, the method of discontinuous single shot shooting shared exactly the same technique problems of film. Shooting with editing in mind became an essential part of that technique. Composition, size of shot, camera movement, camera position and lens-angle had to be carefully selected in order to facilitate a final 'seamless' string of edited images.

The extensive use of video portable cameras especially in news and actuality programmes, was also responsible for a change in compositional style. The ability to rapidly position a lightweight video camera broke down the conventions established with turret cameras. A style evolved, particularly in programmes aimed at young people, where the camera was constantly kept on the move. Although some compositional conventions were retained, the prime intention was to inject excitement and pace by nervous, erratic camera movement.

In its extreme form, it was similar to the subjective style of the camera as an actor with other participants in the production treating it as a person. In this style, if someone spoke out of frame, the camera would swerve to find them. It moved around discussions and in and out of groups with very little attempt (or inclination) to disguise the movement. This was a studied attempt to avoid conventional production technique in an endeavour to create a different visual appearance to that seen in mainstream television.

Hot heads and remote controlled cameras

One of the limitations of development shots that attempted to cover a wide range of movement in space was the need for the camera to be manned. This required the crane to carry the weight of the cameraman and camera on a boom arm that was counterbalanced and positioned in space by a tracker. The whole of this weight was mounted on a moving platform often driven by a motor. This type of crane was a large and sometimes limited device to produce camera movement.

The development of the remote controlled lightweight camera mounted on a much lighter dolly using a remote controlled 'hot head' (a generic title for a remotely controlled pan/tilt head) allowed camera developments that were not possible with the traditional crane design. The range of the lightweight boom arms were much greater and could be swung into former inaccessible positions such as over the top of audiences or in high angle positions within a set. A greater speed of movement in shot development became possible and a whole new range of fluid compositions became commonplace.

Remote controlled cameras and pedestals were introduced into news studios and allowed one individual to control a number of cameras from a control room position. Robotic cameras could be pre-programmed to provide a range of shots at the touch of a button and to re-position in the studio. A timed pre-set zoom movement could be created that reframed the shot utilizing pivot points (see Chapter 10, Movement). The 'remoteness' of this type of camera operation precludes some types of production contribution provided by a manned camera.

Summary

The origins of contemporary camerawork are to be found in changes in painting styles over the last 500 years, in the influence of still photography and in changes in the style and the technology of film and television production. The influence of past solutions to visual problems conditions much of current practice.

Photography in the nineteenth century developed a compositional style of the instantaneous framing of an everyday event. The most effective 'freeze frame' images of motion arrested use the tension between subjects moving apart, and subject and their relationship to their surroundings. When the frame cuts a figure there is the implication that the frame position is arbitrary, that the scene is endless and a portion of the event just happened to be cut by the frame at that point by chance.

The development of film technique involved finding methods of changing shot without distracting the audience. A number of 'invisible' techniques were discovered and became the standard conventions of film making and later television. These included continuity cutting and parallel action cutting, variation in shot size and not crossing 'the line', matching camera movement to action, lighting for mood, glamour and atmosphere and editing for pace and variety. The guiding concept that connected all these developing techniques of camera movement and shot change was the need to persuade the audience that they were watching continuous action in real time. This required the mechanics of film making to be hidden from the audience – to be invisible. Expertly used, they were invisible and yet provided the narrative with pace, excitement and variety. These criteria are still valid and much of the pioneering work in the first decades of the century remains intact in current camera technique.

Standard television multi-camera conventions grew out of film technique and the same objectives of disguising technique in order to suspend disbelief in the viewer was adopted. The problem for actuality television was not to recreate 'real time' as in discontinuous film shooting but to meld together multi-camera shooting of an actuality event so that, for example, change of camera angle or cutting between different shot sizes was not obtrusive and distracting to the viewer. The aim once again was towards an 'invisible technique'.

9
Staging

Where shall I stand?

Throughout this book, phrases have been used such as pictorial unity, balanced composition, emphasizing the main subject of interest, etc. Nowhere is this search for picture integration more commonplace and exacting than in the figure/background staging dilemma. As many film and television images consist of faces or figures in a setting, much of the time, cameramen are involved in finding solutions to the visual problem of combining a foreground subject with its background.

We discussed in the figure/ground section how the main subject of interest in an image cannot exist without a background and that often there must be some visual design method to connect the main subject to its 'ground' even though this may be featureless. A plain backing may be sufficient to emphasize the subject, but more usually there is a need to set the subject in context – to provide a setting which will reinforce or comment on the subject. The content of the setting provides atmosphere, mood and information and acts as a powerful reinforcer of the presentation of the main subject of interest. Equally important is the integration of the background with the main subject to provide a unified image.

What is staging?

Blocking movement or staging action refers to the initial setting up of a shot where actor/presenter position and movement is plotted. With the single camera/single shot technique, the complete action for the shot can be seen before camera position, camera movement and lens is decided and the final framing agreed. This should achieve the precise composition that is required because a great deal of control can be exercised in the positioning of actor/presenter to background and the control of background. Essentially, the visual elements that make up the shot can be arranged to achieve the objective of the shot.

This is not dissimilar to the methods painters use to achieve an integrated image. Apart from those few artists who strive for a perfect replication of the scene in view, the design of a painting is achieved by control of the chosen visual components, placing every element where it works for the complete composition.

Although there has always been a great deal of discussion on what constitutes good design, artists have more control over the design of the painting than a cameraman because they have the ability to fashion each visual element to enhance the unity of the image.

Unless the style of painting requires a literal record of the field of view, artists have the ability to arrange and rearrange the painted area so that overall, they achieve the composition they are searching for. Although a great deal of image manipulation can be achieved with lens and camera position, in general, cameramen have to deal with a 'found' visual situation and attempt by lighting and actor positioning to achieve visual control of the whole frame.

In the mid-nineteenth century, early photographers had ambitions to control all the elements of a photographic image and spent a great deal of time setting up and copying academic compositions borrowed from painting. The results were unconvincing, posed freeze frames which soon dropped out of fashion along with the paintings they were attempting to emulate.

Film and television have the added compositional element of subject movement and the tradition of recording the 'real' world. With a few exceptions, the majority of narrative film and television productions stage the dreams, fantasies and desires of the protagonists in the dramas against recognizable slices of location or set. Even though the plots may involve bizarre and fantastic developments, in general, they are played out against settings which contain solid, known objects easily identified by the audience.

Visual story telling therefore has the requirement for tightly designed images created in the choice of set design, costume, make-up, staging, lighting and camera angle. With such a degree of control, the implication is that every image chosen is the result of a production decision. There should be no lucky accidents although the history of film and television camerawork has numerous examples to the contrary.

The American cinematographer Conrad Hall, for example, noticed when setting up a shot for 'In Cold Blood' (1967) that light passing through artificial rain dripping down a set window was casting a shadow of a 'tear' rolling down the cheeks of the artiste in close-up who was remembering his past (sad) life. This simple visual accident was immediately incorporated into the shot. Gordon Willis shooting 'The Godfather' (1972) used top lighting to help reduce Brando's heavy jowls. This resulted in Brando's eyes being in shadow and intensified the menace of the character.

Staging action for a number of television cameras to shoot continuously, however, often requires a great deal of compromise between the ideal for each shot and what in practice can be achieved. Multi-camera television coverage requires pre-planning of set or location, set design, lighting and a camera script with details of all planned shots. For complex programmes such as drama, there will also be extensive pre-rehearsal of artistes involved where interpretation and action is devised and plotted.

Figure 9.1 Camera 3 has a strong vertical line in the background of its shot. If the camera crabs left to get rid of it, the window line will enter camera right. If the camera crabs right, the foreground figure will start to mask the upstage artiste. Repositioning the table will affect other shots. Sometimes, there is not a great deal of adjustment available for the optimum positioning of actor and background with continuous multi-camera shooting. Any reposition of an actor for one camera will affect the framing of another camera.

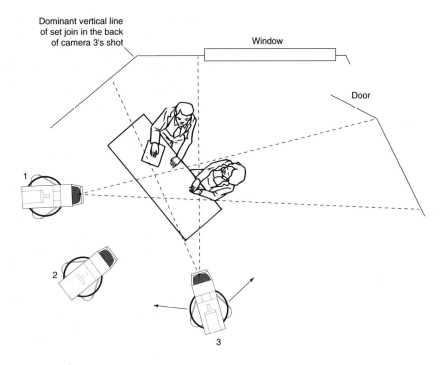

Once in the studio or at the location, each shot will be blocked and then a run through of the scene will test the practicalities and the problems of the camera script. With continuous multi-camera shooting, there is not a great deal of adjustment available for the optimum positioning of actor and background. Any repositioning of the actor for one camera will affect the framing of another camera. Reasonable compromises are sought but the perfection of the single shot/single camera framing are often not a practical option. A dozen small corrections that would have been made for single camera shooting such as lighting, background set changes and artist positioning are not always possible if continuous action is covered by multi-cameras. The tendency in multi-camera television shooting is for shot size to have greater importance and precedence over the search for the integrated image that is possible with single shot recording.

Framing up a shot of inanimate objects is easier and involves finding the right position in space for the lens with the right lens-angle and then devising the lighting, balance and frame. If the visual elements in the frame are small enough to rearrange, then good composition can be achieved by placing each item in an optimum position for visual unity.

Staging people and staging action

If good composition can only be achieved by control of the visual elements, how is it possible to re-order the visual elements in a shot to create a dynamic composition? In the chapter on perspective, we discussed ways of adjusting the camera to subject relationship in order to produce dynamic compositions. Control of the skeleton of the picture can be ordered by choice of lens, camera position and camera distance from subject.

Frequently, in television and film, the principal subjects in the frame are people. In a controlled situation where the artist can be positioned with relationship to the lens, there is frequently an optimum position which gives the best composition with that specific background and artist. Best in this context means the most appropriate relationships for the message that is to be communicated.

A common relationship in television news/factual programming is the reporter with the 'over my left shoulder World War Three has just broken out' shot. This combination of reporter delivering a piece to camera with the suggestion or flavour of the content of the piece in the background is commonplace but frequently produces awkward framing.

If the reportage concerns a civil catastrophe or strong visual activity in the background then a combined image will result in divided interest between reporter and the background event. What may be intended as background 'atmosphere' for the 'piece to camera' often develops into a split screen with a double shot obliging the viewer to constantly shift their attention between foreground and background. The two centres of interest – reporter and background – are usually caused because of the tight framing of the reporter. The close size of shot and the talking to camera creates a separation, a detachment from the glimpsed events taking place outside the intimacy established between reporter and viewer. Talking to the lens creates the effect of standing outside the situation being reported, of taking a detached, objective view of the type of extraordinary event that would normally have overwhelmed and involved an observer.

Journalistic values are claimed to be based on the search for objectivity, of the seeking after fact as opposed to comment or opinion but paradoxically, this 'objectivity' is often accompanied by powerful, emotional images that are intended to grab and involve the audience's attention. The subjective, emotionally involving images of human suffering or despair are sometimes combined, in an uneasy alliance, with a 'factual' piece to camera.

The most neutral and objective image would appear to be the fashion for posing the journalist against a sign or logo. Over the shoulder of the reporter is seen a notice which may say 'Home Office', 'Scotland Yard', 'Treasury', etc.

This type of shot often fails to work as the background rectangle sign fights the foreground reporter as the main subject of interest. Divided interest seems to appeal to literal minded journalists accustomed to working with print. The background sign appeals to them because they believe it reinforces the story whereas in fact a divided interest image is a distraction.

The same divided interest is carried over into the news bulletin where the newsreader is pushed out of the frame by a programme logo or generic title. This stale visual arrangement is an awkward composition that has achieved acceptability by constant repetition (Figure 9.2).

Interviews

A recurring news and feature item is the location interior interview. It usually requires shots of the interviewee seated in their office or house being questioned by a presenter.

Figure 9.2

There are a number of factors in deciding camera position and interview position including:

- Does the interview position allow a variety of shot to sustain a long interview if required?
- Can the relationship of the people be shown?
- Is the environment of the interviewee important to the interview? Does the background to the shot give more information?
- Is there a comfortable distance between participants for them to relate to each other?
- Is there space and how convenient is it to relight and reposition for reverses?
- Do windows need to be in shot?
- The colour temperature difference and balance between daylight entering from windows and the light provided by added lamps.

If there is complete control over the subject position then look for a background which will draw attention to the subject, will balance out the main subject (e.g. offset framing) and will hint at explanation of the subject either by mood, atmosphere or information.

Movement within the shot and lens-angle

A two-dimensional film or television image of three-dimensional space can involve compromise between action and the requirements of the camera. A common adjustment is the speed of the actor movement to the size of the shot or the lens-angle in use.

A small movement in a close-up can be the equivalent of a big movement in long shot. A full figure, three pace walk towards a wide angle lens will create a much bigger change in size than the equivalent full figure walk towards a 25° lens. The 'internal space' of the lens in use becomes a critical consideration when staging action for the camera (Figures 9.3a and 9.3b).

Actor movement which is motivated by the story line is often required to be modified by the demands of the specific lens in use. One of the most common adjustments is the speed of a rise from a chair which may need to be covered in close-up. A normal rise will often appear frantic contained in a tight shot and is frequently slowed down. This also helps with the problem of achieving good framing when covering a fast moving subject on a tight lens.

Another common development shot is keeping a foreground artiste or object in shot while crabbing to follow the background

Figure 9.3 The same size of foreground subject achieved with a narrow angle lens (a) and a wide angle lens (b).

(a)   (b)

movement of another actor. This is fairly straightforward using a wide angle lens if the camera position is tight to the foreground subject as this allows the arc of the crab to be relatively short. A few feet of camera movement will accommodate a 10 ft change of position of a background artist. If a longer lens is used, for the same size foreground image, the camera is much further back and the arc of the crabbing line now becomes considerably extended in order to keep the same background actor movement in shot (Figures 9.4a and 9.4b). Using a narrower lens also alters the apparent movement of the camera as less background scenery is covered by the sweep of the lens.

The internal space of a shot

The internal space of the shot is a subtle but important part of the look, mood and atmosphere of the shot. As we have seen, when three-dimensional objects are converted into a flat two-dimensional image, size relationships will be controlled by camera distance to subject and lens-angle. A small room can appear large using a wide angle lens and a large room can appear cramped and condensed using a long lens.

A medium shot of an actor can be achieved using a lens-angle that varies between more than 75° down to less than 5°. The wider angles will produce possible distortion of features or exaggerated body movement but the crucial distinction between using these range of lens-angles is that to keep the same size medium shot, the camera will move further and further back from the main subject as the lens-angle is decreased. This will alter the size relationship between foreground and background – the internal space of the shot – will altered.

Production style and lens-angle

So what lens-angle should be selected? This will depend on the mood or feel of the shot and the action that it is to contain. For visual continuity during a scene, or even for the whole production, it would seem to be necessary to keep within a limited range of lens-angles. One style of production consistently uses a wide angle lens producing a series of shots which emphasize movement towards or away from the lens giving a great deal of internal space to the shots, often accompanied by a low camera height emphasizing ceilings and dynamic converging lines of walls, building, etc.

Another 'internal space' style is to use long lenses producing compressed space, extended movement towards and away from the camera and a general mood of claustrophobia. Frequently this style is accompanied by a lack of 'geography' shots – shots which provide information about setting or locale. Shot in tight close-up, the action is followed without revealing the location, resulting in a series of images with swirling backgrounds which generates pace without information. The viewer is sucked into the mystery and teased with a lack of precise visual clues as to the surroundings.

The choice of the lens-angle is therefore dependent on how the action is to be staged and the visual style that is required.

The narrower the lens-angle the more difficult it becomes to achieve smooth and fluid camera development and movement. The

Figure 9.4 (a) A common development shot is to hold a two shot of foreground actor (C) while actor A walks to B. If the camera position is tight to the foreground subject (C) the arc of the crab is relatively short. (b) If a longer lens is used, for the same size foreground image, the camera is much further back and the arc of the crabbing line now becomes considerably extended in order to keep the same background actor movement in shot.

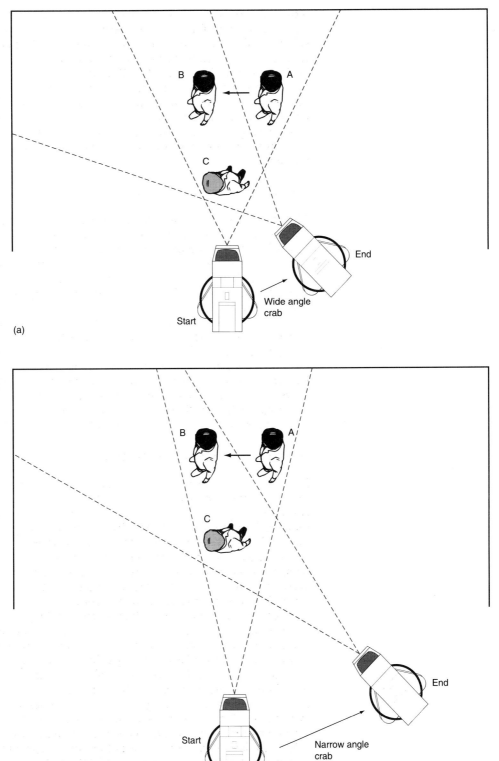

(a)

(b)

camera has to travel further to achieve size change or movement on a narrow lens than on a wide angle; is more prone to movement vibration or unsteadiness on very narrow angles; and requires larger and more precise focus pulls.

Camera movement must have visual elements that change their relationship depending on camera position. A crab around a subject set against a featureless background will provide slight indication of change of viewpoint. The same movement with the subject set against a varied and broken background now has markers to indicate the change of viewpoint. If foreground features sweep across the frame there are even more indicators that the viewpoint is changing and the movement (if that is what is required) becomes more dominant and visual.

Camera movement using a narrow lens has a distinct visual quality but requires greater operational precision than wide angle movement, which is easier to achieve and where there is great deal more movement in the frame for the distance covered.

The internal space of a shot often underlines the emotional quality of the scene. 'Normal' perspective (see Chapter 3) for establishing shots is often used where the intention is to plainly and straightforwardly describe the locale. A condensed or an expanded space on the other hand may help to suggest the mood or atmosphere of the action.

The choice of lens-angle and resulting composition should not be accidental unless, as is frequently too often the case, camera position and angle is a *fait accompli* created by a multi-camera compromise.

Control of background

A small area of background can be controlled by lighting or by limiting the depth of field by an ND (neutral density) filter but the greatest control is by choice of camera position, lens-angle, camera distance and foreground subject position. Consideration must also be given to how the shot will be intercut and often a matching background of similar tonal range, colour and contrast has to be chosen to avoid a mismatch when intercutting.

Too large a tonal range between intercut backgrounds will result in obtrusive and very visible cuts. Visual continuity of elements such as direction of light, similar zones of focus and the continuity of background movement (e.g. crowds, traffic, etc.) in intercut shots have also to be checked.

Figure composition

Single figure composition

The single figure occurs constantly in film and television framing. There appears to be two aspects that affect its relationship with the setting (other elements will be discussed in the appropriate sections). With a simple or plain background, the figure should be in contact with one or two edges of the frame in order to achieve unity with the image. With a shot closer than full figure this is obviously inevitable. If the context of the shot allows, a side-lit portraiture enables the darker side of the face to set up a relationship with the background. Another visual solution is to find a balancing relationship with background forms or light (using shadow), similar shapes or colour. A single figure is often used to show scale in a landscape and will be identified by movement even if the figure is dominated by the location.

The most useful staging to integrate offset figures with their background is to get the presenter to stand with his or her body turned into the frame rather than square-on to camera. If the shoulder line points into the background then there is a natural lead-in which connects background to foreground.

Two figure composition

Two people in a frame can quickly lead to a 'divided interest' composition unless one of them is made more dominant. This can be achieved by unequal size or position in frame or simply having one person with their back to camera. There are many standard two-shot stagings ranging from a larger foreground figure contrasted with a smaller sized background figure, over-the-shoulder two-shots, three-quarter two-shot, etc. Other methods of switching attention between two figures in the same frame is by dialogue, movement or lighting.

Multi-figure compositions

Circles, pyramid and oval groupings are classical solutions to binding together three, four or more subjects. Using the outline shapes of heads and arms and legs to guide the eye around the simple geometric forms, individuals are merged into a coherent composition. It is important to set a focus point (the main subject) within the group and then build the most appropriate shape to emphasize that point.

Individuals in the group may be active or passive in their relationship to the overall composition. Staging people with their backs to camera or in three-quarter profile weakens their importance. Placing people on the focus of a leading line formed by the group's outline shape or other strong directional line, will strengthen their importance. Balancing two people against one within a pyramid grouping is another standard solution to control attention (Figure 9.5).

Figure 9.5 A shot from the 'The Maltese Falcon' showing a circular arrangement of faces to bind together a group shot.

Working at speed

Because of the wide range of techniques that are employed in film and television production it is not possible or desirable to itemize a set of compositional do's and dont's that will cover all situations. Certain basic conventions can be identified that are in use across a wide spectrum of camerawork but in general, as with the choice of camera equipment, it is 'horses for courses'. One specialist area of programming or film making will evolve a certain way of working which suits the requirements of that technique. Other types of production would find these conventions restricting or superfluous.

Actuality programming – working live or recording as live (i.e. no re-takes) all have one technique in common. Live action demands a stream of continuous pictures which means that each cameraman is required to frame up their shots at speed. Occasionally they may have time to reposition the camera without haste and to take time out to consider the precise framing of a shot. This is a rare and infrequent luxury in many types of programming such as sport, music or group discussions. Most productions require a continuous variety of shots often linked to a specific event.

The live multi-camera coverage of an orchestral concert, for example, will be camera scripted in sympathy with the piece performed. Depending on the nature of the music and the television treatment decided by the director, there may be in excess of 200–300 plus shots shared between five or more cameras.

Each shot has its designated function in the score and must be ready and framed at the precise bar that it is required. The speed of the camerawork will therefore be synchronized with the music and at times this will entail rapid and continuous shot change. The tempo of the camerawork varies between extremely quick reactions 'off' shot to find the next instrument, to slow camera movement on-shot that reflects the mood of the music. Panning movements have to be synchronized with the number of bars allocated to that shot and must finish exactly on the instrument or group of instruments agreed because possibly, at that point in time, a solo or change of tempo may occur.

This reflex framing with occasionally no time to consciously consider composition, is achieved by relying on habit and the developed feeling for a good picture that instantly oversees the eye/hand co-ordination. If there is no time to consider the image the only thing to do is to rely on experience and training. Live television continuously requires quick compositional decisions.

Camerawork that is carried out in the real time of the event covered often allows no time for any thoughtful consideration about the precise way of framing. There is no opportunity to reorder the visual elements. The most that can be done in the time available is to trim the shot by way of the zoom and a slight jiggle of the framing points.

An example of the instinctive response to movement can be seen in slow motion replays of fast sporting action. The square-on 'slo mo' camera position in cricket coverage is required to follow the ball as soon as it leaves the bat. Sometimes even the batsman does not know which way the ball went. Continuously during the game, the slow motion replays reveal that the cameraman has instinctively followed the ball to a fielder who has gathered the ball and aimed it at the stumps in one fluid movement. The framing seen in slow motion belies the real speed and technique required to follow and keep the ball in the frame and the players involved. It has been judged that the speed of the action is sometimes too fast for the umpires on the field to assess what has happened and they call upon a third umpire in the stadium to adjudicate. He is able to do this by relying on the slow motion replay of the debated incident. High technology does not provide this aid – simply the fast reflexes of cameramen.

In unscripted multi-camera working, one eye has to be kept on what other cameras are offering (through mixed viewfinder or a monitor) in order to provide alternative shots to the shot on transmission. Although most television sports coverage has designated roles for each camera, there are often accompanying incidents such as presentations at the end of the event or 'celebrating' spectator shots which require an ad lib coverage. In group discussion programmes, size of shot must be matched and alternatives available for cutaways.

Summary

Many film and television images consist of faces or figures in a setting. Much of the time, cameramen are involved in finding solutions to the visual problem of combining a foreground subject with its background.

The internal space of the shot is a subtle but important part of the look, mood and atmosphere of the shot. When three-dimensional objects are converted into a flat two-dimensional image, size relationships will be controlled by camera distance to subject and lens-angle. The choice of the lens-angle is therefore dependent on how the action is to be staged and the visual style that is required.

10
Movement

Invisible movement

The camerawork technique practised by the professional TV camera-man – such as stop/start camera movement on action; matching camera movement to subject movement; pivot points on zooms and tracks; matched shots on intercuts – is designed to make 'invisible' the mechanics of programme production. The intention is usually to emphasize subject – picture content – rather than technique.

An old cliché of Hollywood is that 'a good cutter cuts his own throat'. It refers to the invisible technique employed by film editors to stitch together a series of shots so that the audience is unaware that any artifice or craft has been employed. The transition between images is so natural that the techniques used flow past unnoticed. The editor has done such a good job in disguising his or her contribution to the film that their expertise is invisible. If the viewer is unaware of the camerawork then quite often the cameraman has achieved his objective. Like the old Hollywood saying, expert camerawork, whether single or multi-camera, renders the camera-men anonymous.

The antithesis of this is seen in many home videos where hose-piping the camera and zoomitis draws attention to the method of recording the subject and zaps the viewer into visual stupefaction. The drawback of practising an invisible technique is that to the unini-tiated, there is no obvious 'craft'. The cameraman is not only anony-mous, he appears to have made little contribution to the programme.

Camera movement

Two basic conventions with camera movement are firstly to match the movement to action so that the camera move is motivated by the action and is controlled in speed, timing and degree by action.

Secondly, there is a need to maintain good composition throughout the move. A camera move is a visual development that provides new information or creates atmosphere or mood. If the opening and closing frames of a move, such as a zoom in, are the only images that are considered important, then it is probably better to use a cut to change shot rather than a camera move. A camera move should provide new visual interest and there should be no 'dead' area between the first and end image.

Movement that is not motivated by action will be obtrusive and focus attention on the method of recording the image. It will make visible the camera technique employed. It is sometimes the objective of obtrusive camera movement to invigorate content that is considered stale and lacking interest. If there is a lack of confidence in the content of a shot, then possibly it is better to rethink the subject rather than attempting to disguise this weakness by moving attention on to the camera technique employed.

Single camera and multi-camera movement

Film is a record of an event edited and assembled after the event occurs. Live television is a presentation of an event as it occurs. Although camera movement in single and multi-camera shooting share many similarities, they are to some extent conditioned by the differences imposed by the practice of recording a single shot and the practicalities of recording or transmitting a number of shots continuously.

Live, or recorded as live, multi-camera coverage presents an event in real time and requires flexible camera mounts able to provide a variety of shots. In the studio, camera movement can be maximized on or off shot by tracking over level floors. Film and single camera coverage can break the action into single shots and lay tracks and devise movement without the need to compromise or be inhibited by other camera movement.

Staging action for multi-camera continuous coverage requires a great deal more visual compromise than action which is conceived for a single shot. There are limitations on set design and lighting for multi-camera shooting which are easily overcome or simply not a consideration in single shot/single camera recording. In general, because of the constraints of time/budget, multi-camera operation often requires constant minor adjustments to the frame in order to accommodate actor position or staging that could have been re-plotted if time/budget (and the ever present need for multi-camera compromise) was available. (see Chapter 11, Multi-camera drama coverage).

Two types of movement – functional and decorative

Camera movement can be conveniently grouped as functional movement and decorative movement. This over-simplified division will often overlap but if functional movement is reframing to accommodate subject movement, then decorative movement can be defined as a planned, deliberate change of camera position or zoom to provide visual variety, narrative emphasis or new information.

This type of camera movement also includes change of size of shot motivated by dialogue or narrative demands. Frequently, the importance or emotional intensity of a line of dialogue will naturally draw the camera closer but the move has to be handled with sensitivity and feeling and timed to exactly match the emotions expressed. Just as camera movement will be synchronized with the start/stop points of action, movement motivated by dialogue or emotional expression, will be controlled by the timing and nuances of the performance.

Multi-camera actuality coverage requires a great deal of reframing to keep the subject in frame. As subject movement is frequently unplanned, the composition of the shot will need continuous adjustment. This requires a pan and tilt head that can be instantly adjusted in discrete movements. Working with a single camera, a preplanned single shot can be rehearsed and the camera operator can make precise arrangements for subject movement with a geared pan/tilt head if preferred.

Multi-camera coverage requires maximum flexibility with camera movement to follow often unrehearsed action. A common dilemma is when to reframe a subject who is swaying in and out of reasonable framing. The shot may become too tight for a subject who needs to emphasize every point with hand gestures. It is seldom possible to constantly pan to keep someone who is swaying in frame as inevitably an anticipated movement does not happen and the composition becomes unbalanced. If the shot cannot be contained without continuous reframing then the incessant moving background will eventually become a distraction from the main subject of the shot. If the viewer is unaware of the camerawork then quite often the cameraman has achieved his objective. Expert camerawork, whether single or multi-camera, provides invisible camera movement by matching movement to action.

The pan

The simplest camera movement on a static subject is the pan. It is often used in the mistaken idea that it gives visual variety among a number of static shots. Usually, the main use of a pan, apart from keeping a moving subject in frame, is to show relationships.

There is obviously the need to begin a pan with a well-balanced shot that has intrinsic interest in its own right. The second requirement is to find visual elements that allow the pan to flow smoothly and inevitably to the end framing. The end frame must be well balanced and again of intrinsic interest. The pan alerts the viewer that the camera is moving to reveal some image of importance or interest. If this anticipation is denied and the end framing is quickly cut away from because it contains no visual interest, then the total movement has been wasted.

The speed of a panning shot must be matched to content. Panning fast over complex detail produces irritation – it is impossible to take in the information. Panning slowly over large, unbroken, plain areas may provoke boredom. It is almost always necessary to help with the visual change by finding some visual connection between first and last composition. Panning with movement, along lines, edges or any horizontal or vertical visual link usually disguises the transition and leads the eye naturally to the next point of interest. The reverse of this technique is frequently seen in the 'pan and scan' conversion of widescreen films to 4×3 television screens. The 4×3 framing oscillates from one side of the original widescreen to the other with no visual motivation other than change of dialogue location. This ersatz 'panning' is obtrusive and clumsy.

The rate of movement may alter during a camera move. If the composition is such that the subject is close to the edge of the frame when they begin their move, it will be necessary to make a swift adjustment of the frame to give them 'walking' room before settling down to the movement framing. Likewise, at the end of the move, the final frame may have to be arrived at by a similar speedier reframing of the subject to achieve a balanced final frame. If possible, the action should be staged to avoid sudden changes of pace and to provide a fluid, smooth movement.

Pivot points

A common mistake with users of domestic camcorders is to centre the subject of interest in the frame and then to zoom towards them keeping the subject the same distance from all four sides of the frame. The visual effect is as if the frame implodes in on them from all sides.

A more pleasing visual movement is to keep two sides of the frame at the same distance from the subject for the whole of the movement. This is achieved in a track or a zoom by preselecting a pivot point in the composition which is usually the main subject of interest and whilst maintaining their position at a set distance from two adjacent sides of the frame, allow the other two sides of the frame to change their relative position to the subject. This allows the subject image to grow progressively larger (or smaller) within the frame whilst avoiding the impression of the frame contracting in towards them (Figure 10.1).

Figure 10.1 Preselect one or two adjacent sides of the frame to the main subject of the zoom and whilst maintaining their position at a set distance from the main subject of the zoom allow the other two sides of the frame to change their relative position to the subject. Keep the same relationship of the adjacent frame edge to the selected subject during the whole of the zoom movement.

The point that is chosen to be held stationary in the frame is called the pivot point. Using a *pivot point* allows the subject image to grow progressively larger (or smaller) within the frame whilst avoiding the impression of the frame contracting in towards them.

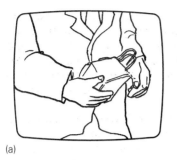

(a)

(b)

(c)

Figure 10.2 An extended development shot in the opening sequence of 'Touch of Evil' (1958). (a) Close-up of timer of bomb being set in someone's hands; (b) bomb being placed in boot of car; (c) camera cranes up to see couple walk to the car; (d) the car passes the principal characters and the camera follows them ... (e) ... to the frontier post where the car with the bomb draws alongside.

(d)

(e)

It may be necessary on a combined track and crabbing movement to change this pivot point during the move but again as in all camera techniques, the changeover to a different pivot point must be subtle, unobtrusive and controlled by the main subject of interest.

The development shot

Tracking or crabbing the camera to emphasize another visual element in the frame is a standard convention that has been used for many years. A development shot, as the name implies, is a shot which smoothly and unobtrusively moves towards a new viewpoint. It can start with a composition that emphasizes one set of visual elements and then moves, motivated by action or driven by the audience's curiosity, to an image that emphasizes another set of visual elements. In dramatic terms, it has no real equivalent in theatre or literature and when staging, pace and execution are fully integrated it can provide the most visually exciting images.

To achieve its greatest impact, a development often requires foreground elements to wipe across frame to emphasize movement; it requires a progressive change of viewpoint from its starting position; and it needs a main subject of interest that can be followed through various dynamic compositions. Although the movement must be fluid and changing, it requires a continuing revelation of dynamic images.

The opening shot of 'Touch of Evil' (1958) directed by Orson Welles shows a package being placed in the boot of a parked car. People enter the car and the camera cranes up and away over the roof of a house as the car pulls away. Tracking across a street the camera finds another couple walking and then follows the car and the couple as they walk though a Mexican frontier town. The car and the walking couple constantly switch positions as the main subject of

(a)

(b)

(c)

Figure 10.3 (a)(b)(c) Keeping the subject in mid-shot, the camera tracks out while zooming in to keep the subject image the same size. Because of the increasing camera distance and narrower lens-angle, a smaller and smaller portion of the background is included in the frame. The visual effect is to freeze the subject in space as the background apparently flows out either side of the frame.

interest before the car reaches the frontier customs post and explodes. This continuous development lasting a minute of screen time allows the plot to be established whilst creating atmosphere and excitement all contained in one fluid exciting development. Actor movement and camera movement need to be perfectly choreographed by the director to achieve such visual cohesion (Figures 10.2a–10.2e).

Compositional impact can also be achieved by combining unexpected perspective characteristics. In Stephen Spielberg's 'Jaws' (1975), the sheriff of a seaside town has been anticipating the return of the man-eating shark and suddenly hears screams from the beach. Keeping him in mid-shot, the camera tracks and zooms, which keeps his image the same size but, because of the changing camera distance, progressively shows a background to foreground size ratio change. The visual effect is to freeze him in space while the background is apparently in flux. The same double movement of camera and zoom was used by Alfred Hitchcock in 'Vertigo'.

Static camera – moving subject

Lens-angle, camera distance and camera height will dictate the characteristics of a moving subject composition. On a long lens with the subject at a distance from the camera, space will be compressed and movement will appear disproportionally small compared to image size. For example, a subject can walk ten paces on a long lens in mid-shot and hardly register a change in size. This contradicts our normal perception of perspective change and sets up a surreal 'running on the spot' feel to the image.

A close position with a wide angle lens will accentuate movement and any movement towards the camera will make the subject change size disproportionately to the actual movement taken. Action that is corner to corner will be more dynamic than action which sweeps horizontally across the frame.

Moving camera – moving subject

One of the most common forms of moving camera/moving subject shot is to follow, in the same size shot, a subject walking or driving. A popular convention is the parallel tracking shot where two people in conversation walk with the camera crabbing with them often slightly ahead so that both faces are seen. For this technique to be 'invisible' the frame must be steady, horizontally level and the same size shot maintained over most of the move. The effect is as if the audience was a third person walking with them and listening in to their conversation.

A number of visual variations are to be found which rely on what is a static foreground of main subject whilst the background moves. People in cars, trains even glass lifts can be held framed in static shot while the background moves behind them.

Moving the camera whilst the subject size alters can be more difficult to handle. Unless there are other visual elements moving in and out of the frame, the change in size of the subject can appear as if the camera is unable to keep up or is gaining on the subject. When the movement is across the frame as in a crabbing shot then change

Figure 10.4 (a) At the start of the track in, the foreground subject is twice as large as the background subject. (b) At the end of the track in, the foreground subject is more than three times as large as the background subject. (c) At the start of the zoom in, the foreground subject is twice as large as the background subject. (d) At the end of the zoom in, the foreground subject is still twice as large as the background subject. There has been no change in the perspective of mass.

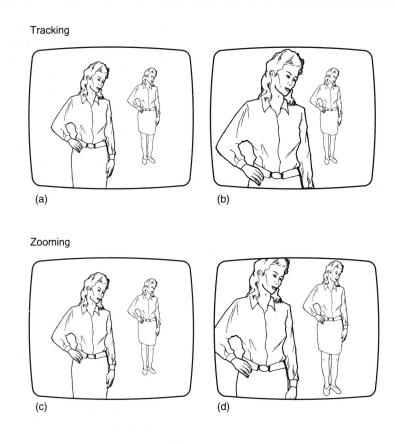

Tracking

(a)   (b)

Zooming

(c)   (d)

of size may not be so apparent and is visually acceptable.

The distinction between tracking and zooming

As we have seen in the section on perspective, moving the camera towards or away from the subject alters the size relationships between foreground and background objects. The perspective of mass changes in a similar way to our own perceptual experience when we move towards or away from an object. Tracking the camera therefore not only conforms to our normal visual expectations but sets up interesting re-arrangements of all the visual elements in the camera's field of view. Changing the camera distance alters all the image size relationships apart from very distant objects near or on the horizon. The size of a range of hills remain unaffected no matter how far we travel towards them until we reach a critical distance where we have a part of the hills as foreground with which to compare a background.

The greatest impression of movement can be observed by using a wide angle lens and tracking between similar size objects such as a row of trees on each side of a road. The apparent size of each tree to its neighbour changes dramatically as it approaches the lens. There is a constant visual flow of size ratio expansion as we track down the road.

Zooming along the road between rows of trees does not have anything like the same visual dynamics. The camera does not move and therefore there is no change in size relationships. The zoom simply magnifies the central portion of the field of view preserving the existing size relationships. They remain unaltered as in a still photograph when a portion of it is enlarged. The perspective of mass is decided by the camera distance and zooming simply expands or contracts a portion of the field of view.

The feeling of flatness or deadness of a zoom is because there is no anticipated change to the perspective of mass which in normal perception accompanies changes in magnification or diminution of subject. This compositional inertia can be disguised by building in a camera move such as a pan with action or even a crabbing movement to accompany a zoom. The camera movement provides some relational changes to the visual elements that the zoom is magnifying.

Maintaining good composition when moving

When tracking, it is often necessary to adjust the height of the camera particularly when moving into the human figure. In shots closer than full figure, lens height is often eye-height but when the camera is further away, depending on the shot, the lens-height is usually lower to reduce the amount of floor/ground in shot. A low lens-height places emphasis on the subject by avoiding distracting foreground level surfaces such as roads, grass or floor. Like all 'rules of thumb', this convention is probably ignored more than it is employed but changes in lens height often accompany tracking movements in order to bring emphasis on to the main subject.

Another reason for altering the lens height when tracking into the subject is to enhance the appearance of actors/actresses by shooting slightly down on faces, rather than shooting up and emphasizing jaw lines and double chins, etc.

Using dominant lines and movement

One of the ways of achieving 'invisible' movement is to use dominant horizontal, vertical or angled lines to pan along in order to move to a new viewpoint. Panning on lines in the frame allows visual continuity between two images and appears to provide a satisfactory visual link. The same visual link can be achieved by using movement within the frame to allow a pan or a camera movement from one composition to another. The most common convention in an establishing shot is to follow a person across the set or location, to allow new information about the geography of the setting as the shot develops. The person the camera follows may be unimportant but is used to visually take the camera from a starting composition to possibly the main subject.

Speed of movement matched to mood and content

It is important to understand the content of a moving shot and if the camera movement, pan or zoom is too fast then the information will be unreadable. If the development is too fast for content then there will be a mismatch of a mood. The speed of a pan across a symphony orchestra playing a slow majestic piece will be at a different speed to the pan across when it is at full gallop. Speed of movement must match mood and content. If it is required to be discreet and invisible then movement must begin when the action begins and end when the action ends. A crane or tilt up with a person rising must not anticipate the move neither must it be late in catching up with the move. Any movement that is bursting to get out of the frame must either be allowed some camera movement to accommodate it or there is a need for a shot change.

Summary

Camerawork technique – such as stop/start camera movement on action; matching camera movement to subject movement; pivot points on zooms and tracks; matched shots on intercuts – is designed to make 'invisible' the mechanics of programme production. The objective is usually to emphasize the subject – *picture content* – rather than camera technique.

Two basic conventions with camera movement are firstly to match the movement to the action so that the camera move is motivated by the action and is controlled in speed, timing and degree by action. Secondly, there is a need to maintain good composition throughout the move. A camera move should provide new visual interest and there should be no 'dead' area between the first and end image of the movement.

Functional movement is reframing to accommodate subject movement. *Decorative* movement can be defined as a planned, deliberate change of camera position or zoom to provide visual variety, narrative emphasis or new information. Just as camera movement will be synchronized with the start/stop points of action, movement motivated by dialogue or emotional expression, will be controlled by the timing and nuances of the performance.

11
Context

Post-production and composition

One aspect of the composition of a shot is to consider how it will relate to the preceding and succeeding shots. If a production allows pre-planning, a camera script or storyboard will have been blocked-out and the structure of each sequence and how shots are to be cut together will be roughly known or even precisely planned. Additional cover shots will be composed and devised with the original scripted shots in mind.

In factual programming, however, the order of a particular sequence of shots may be unknown at the time of recording. The editor requires from the cameraman maximum flexibility with material supplied and the nucleus of a structure. A 'ground plan' of a potential sequence of shots is often mentally sketched out in order to assist in the edit. Edit-point requirements such as change in angle and shot size, subject movement, camera movement and continuity have to be considered and provided for to enable the footage to be assembled in a coherent stream of images. Shooting with editing in mind is therefore essential (Figure 11.1).

Unscripted shot structure

Much of the 'magazine' type item location work may not be scripted. There may be a rough treatment outlined by the presenter or a written brief on what the item should cover but an interview may open up new aspects of the story. Without pre-planning or a shot-list, camera technique will often revert to tried and trusted formulas. Telling a story in pictures is as old as the first efforts in film making.

From the general to the particular

A safe general rule is to move from the general to the particular – from wide shot to close-up. A general view (GV) to show relationships and to set the scene and then to make the important points

Exit left   Cut to...   Enter right

Rise from chair; hold static frame   Cut to...   The rise is repeated in static frame wide shot

Medium shot holding object   Cut to...   Close–up of object must be held in the
                                                        same way as position of hand in medium shot

Figure 11.1 Editing conversions.

with the detail of close-ups. There must be a reason in editing to change shot and the cameraman has to provide a diversity of material to provide a cutting point.

Basic advice for news coverage

- Change of shot must be substantial either in camera position or in shot size.
- Provide the editor with a higher proportion of static shots to camera movement. It is difficult to cut between pans and zooms until they steady to a static frame and hold.
- Try to find relevant but non-specific shots so that voice-over information to set the scene or report can be dubbed on after the script has been prepared.

Information

Information shots are specific. They refer to a unique event – the wreckage of a car crash, someone scoring a goal, a political speech. They are often non-repeatable. The crashed car is towed away, the politician moves on. The topicality of an event means that the camera technique must be precise and reliable, responding to the event with quick reflexes. There is often no opportunity for retakes.

Decoration

Decorative shots are non-specific. They are often shot simply to give visual padding to the story. A typical example is a shot of an interviewee walking in a location before an interview. This shot allows the dubbed voice-over to identify who the interviewee is and possibly their attitude to the subject. The duration of the shot needs to be long enough to allow information that is not featured in the interview to be added as a voice-over. The interviewee leaves the frame at the end of the shot to provide a cutting point to the interview.

Structure

Most location items will have a mixture of this type of informative and decorative shots. It is part of the cameraman's craft to provide the editor/presenter with a variety of options but to keep the shooting ratio in proportion to the editing time available. Information shots are usually straightforward records of the incident or object. If it is technically competent, the information shot requires no more than variety in size and reasonable framing. Decorative shots require a knowledge of television technique and the ability to exploit video and lens characteristics.

Editing requirements

There are a number of editing requirements which will have a bearing on the composition of a shot if a camera script has not been prepared (e.g. news and some documentaries).

Brevity and significance

The value of a shot is its relevance to the story in hand. One single fifteen-second shot may sum up the item but be superfluous in any other context. Check that the vital shots are provided and at the right length before offering visual decoration to the item. Editing for news means reducing to essentials. Make certain that shot length allows for brevity in editing and the relevant cutaways are provided for interviews.

Variety of shot

In order to compress an item to essential information, the editor requires a variety of options. This means a variety of relevant shots in order to restructure a continuous event (e.g. a football match, a conference speech) and to reduce its original time scale to the running order requirement. A continuous twenty-minute MCU of a speaker without audience or relevant cutaways will inevitably lead to a jump cut if more than one portion of the speech is required. Take the opportunity during a pause, which may signal a new topic, or on applause to change the size of shot. Only 'keynote' sentences will be used and a difference in shot size at these points will avoid irrelevant cutaways to shorten the item. Pans, zooms and tilts can be used in a number of ways if the shot is held for five seconds or more before the start and at the end of the camera movement.

Technical competence

There is very little point in providing a number of shots if they are unusable due to wrong exposure or if they are out of focus or the colour temperature is incorrect or if they are shaky and badly framed and important action begins before the recording is sufficiently stable to make an edit.

Continuity

Be aware of possible continuity mismatch between shots in background as well as foreground information. As well as changes over time (weather, light, face tones) watch for changing background action that will prevent intercutting. Avoid staging interviews against significant movement (e.g. a crowd emptying from an arena or a prominent working crane) as background continuity mismatch may prevent the interview being shortened. If possible, have different parts of the background in the singles and two shots if there is significant continuity of movement in the background or choose a static, neutral background.

   Keep a check on the position of coats, hats, clip-on microphones, attitudes of body and head on singles so that they can be matched on two shots.

Speed of access

A large portion of an editing session can be taken up simply finding the relevant shot. Shuttling back and forth between different tapes is time consuming and the edit is greatly speeded up if thought is given to the order in which shots are recorded whenever this is possible.

Shot size

Avoid similar size shots whether in framing, scale, horizon line, etc. unless you provide a bridging shot. For example, a medium shot of an interviewee will not cut with a tight over-the-shoulder favouring the interviewee in the same medium size shot. Wide shots of sea and boats need to be intercut with closer shots of boats to avoid the horizon line jumping in frame. Make certain that the all-over geometry of a shot is sufficiently different from a similar sized shot of the same subject (e.g. GVs of landscapes). In general, television is a close-up medium. Big wide angle shots do not have the same impact they might have on a larger screen.

Crossing the line

To intercut between individual shots of two people to create the appearance of a normal conversation between them, three simple rules have to be observed. If the interviewee in a single is looking from left to right in the frame then the single of the interviewer must look right to left. Secondly, the shot size and eyeline should match (i.e. they should individually be looking out of the frame at a point where the viewer anticipates the other speaker is standing). Finally, every shot of a sequence should stay the same side of an imaginary line drawn between the speakers unless a cutaway is recorded which allows a reorientation on the opposite side of the old 'line' (e.g. either the speakers re-group or the camera moves on shot).

It is easy to forget eyeline direction when recording questions or 'noddys' after an interview has been recorded particularly with a three-hander or when equipment is being demonstrated or explained. Make certain that the camera stays on one side only of the imaginary line drawn between the interviewer and interviewee.

Leaving frame

Do not always follow the action (especially on 'Royal'/'VIP' items where the temptation is to keep the 'notable' in shot at all times). It can sometimes help in editing if the subject leaves frame (hold the empty frame for a few seconds and on the new shot hold the empty frame before the subject enters) as it enables the editor to choose between cutting or not on a moving subject.

Five-second module

News items tend to be constructed on an approximate five-second module. An example of a running order of a news story might be:

12"	voice-over establishing shots
10"	presenter to camera
10"	voice-over
25"	interview (with cutaways)
7"	voice-over

running time of item: 1 minute 04 seconds.

To allow maximum flexibility for the editor, try to shoot in multiples of five seconds. Keep zooms and pans short. For example

    10"   hold at start of zoom (or pan)
    5/10"   zoom (or pan)
    5/10"   hold at end of movement.

This allows the editor a choice of three shots.

Length of pan

Avoid long panning or development shots. Although it may be difficult, depending on the circumstances, try to begin and end a camera movement cleanly. It is difficult to cut into a shot which creeps into or out of a movement. Be positive when you change framing. Use a tripod whenever possible as unsteady shots are difficult to cut and a distraction to the viewer.

Multi-camera

The value of multi-camera technique is its ability to simultaneously observe a continuous event from a number of different camera positions. A continuous actuality event such as sport, music, state and public events, audience discussion, etc. can be transmitted live or continuously recorded to be transmitted later. Traditional multi-camera technique required each camera's picture to be selected through the vision mixing panel and cut to 'line' (i.e. transmitted or recorded) in accordance with a pre-rehearsed camera script detailing all agreed shots or as a mixture of ad lib shots and pre-planned shots.

In order to comprehensively cover a continuous event such as sport, each camera is assigned a role. Covering a football match for example, one camera will mostly stay wide as a master or safety shot that can be cut to at any time whilst the other cameras will stay close for 'personality' close-ups of individual players. Cameras stick to their assigned role in order to provide the director with a guaranteed appropriate shot at all times otherwise duplication of the same shot occurs.

With the expansion in the use of 'iso' feeds, that is an individual camera's output is continuously recorded as well as being available at the mixing panel, a great amount of flexibility is available in post-production to re-edit the recorded material. Iso (isolated) feeds began as a technique to provided variation of shot for instant 'slo mo' playback at live sports events. Now some non-sport multi-camera productions 'iso' each camera and use post-production to complete the edit.

The basis of multi-camera techniques of composition is very similar to single camera operations except that:

1   Cameramen need good communications between producer and crew and if possible exposure needs to be centrally controlled to match pictures.

Figure 11.2 Standard shot sizes.

BCU (big close up)
Whole face fills screen. Top of frame
cuts forehead. Bottom of frame cuts chin

CU (close up)
Bottom of frame cuts where knot of
tie would be

MCU (medium close up)
Bottom of frame cuts where top of
breast pocket of a jacket would be

MS (medium shot)
Bottom of frame cuts at waist

2   The shots are instantaneously edited and therefore need to be matched in size.
3   The shots need to be coordinated to avoid duplication and to provide variety and cutting points.
4   With a live transmission a shot has to be ready and executed at the instant it is required – not when the cameraman is ready to record.
5   There can be no retakes – camerawork problems are not edited out – they are transmitted.

Working as a team

As we have discussed in the section on the legacy of film technique, the skills and techniques used to make a TV programme should not be apparent to the average television viewer. If the viewer becomes aware of technique it will usually distract from the content of the programme. Camera technique should be invisible and this requires matched and consistent camerawork between all cameras on a multi-camera shoot. Unlike single camerawork where an operator may have his own idiosyncratic ways of framing and personal preferences of shot size, multi-camera work requires cameramen to coordinate their framing and composition to avoid 'jump cuts' between shots (Figure 11.2).

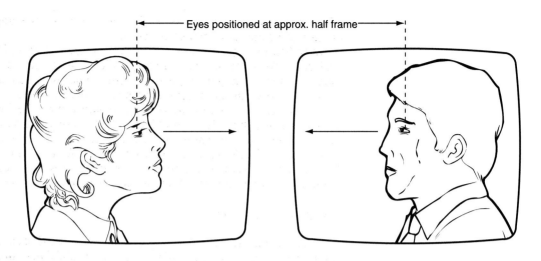

Balanced 'looking room' on intercut shots

Figure 11.3 Looking room.

The description and the framing of the shot needs to be under-stood by cameraman and director (see Figure 11.2) but also:

- headroom should be consistent and adjusted to suit the size of shot;
- the amount of looking room should match for similar sized shots;
- each camera should have the same lens perspective and same camera height when involved in cross cutting on interviews, etc.;
- the pace of camera movement and style of composition should match.

As well as the style of camerawork matching there needs to be a technical match between the cameras. A grey scale line-up before transmission ensures a colour match between cameras – for example the skin tones of a face on different cameras needs to be the same. Also remote control of exposure and black level ensures a better match when intercutting cameras.

Matched shot size and the position in the frame of the subject can be observed and easily adjusted in a multi-camera shoot to allow smooth and 'invisible' cutting. In single camera/single shot coverage there is obviously the need to keep careful records of eyelines, body position, shot-size and other visual indicators in order to achieve visual continuity in post-production.

Style and composition

The style and structure of the composition of a shot also requires a measure of continuity. It was mentioned earlier that the internal space of the shot created by very wide or a very narrow lens-angle must be consistent within a sequence of shots to avoid a mismatch of apparent scene perspective. There is also the need to match shots which have strong line convergencies created by a wide angle lens and a close camera to subject distance.

An individual style of camerawork can be seen as an individual's preference for a certain type of compositional 'look'. Some cameramen will favour a larger proportion of low-angle shots than average. Others devise complex camera movement or seek ambiguous images that tease the viewer into detecting and unravelling the image. In such instances, there is no problem with the compositional match during a sequence of shots because the individual preferences or style will or should remain consistent throughout the production. Problems only occur where someone is dabbling with a number of different 'looks' and a sequence of shots have no visual continuity.

Visual information

A standard convention in building up a sequence of shots is to move from the general to the particular. The wide establishing information shot shows the individual elements in the scene. The closer shots of the individual subjects provide more information and involvement of the audience. The old Hollywood cliché of 'it's the close-up that tells the story, it's the wide shot that sells the picture (show them where the money is)' may have structured thousands of popular, conventional films but it does form the basis of an obvious truth. Unless the film maker wishes to deliberately deceive or confuse the audience, there is inevitably going to be a mixture of wide and close shots to explain, interpret and depict the narrative. The rhythm and arrangement of size of shot independent of content (which it never is) is a three-way creative arrangement between director, cameramen and editor. Creating the right framing, viewpoint, size of shot and visual style will often be the cameraman's contribution.

A close-up will give more information than the same subject in long shot. But the close-up is also a heavy accent – an emphasis which strongly draws the attention of the audience to a specific subject – either a face or even more strongly to an object. The emotional significance of a close shot of a pistol on a table is stronger than a throw-away shot of a car arriving in front of a house.

The narrative 'weight' of a shot is dependent on the size of the shot and also on the composition. Emphasis can be strengthened or lightened depending on the reason for the shot. Visual communication in this sense is similar to language where a shot can be loaded with strong colourful 'adjectives' underlining its significance or can be casually thrown away in neutral tones and left to the audience to judge its significance or make predictions and guess as to its role in the narrative (Figure 11.4).

The context of the shot will control the composition. The 'weight' of its impact has to be carefully considered and the detail and treatment tailored to its role in the production.

The significant image

There is often one key shot within a sequence of shots which sums up or epitomizes what that section of the production is about. The key image may be obvious or its importance may only be revealed by a narrative development that is to occur later.

Figure 11.4 Kuleshov and I made an interesting experiment. We took from some film or other several close-ups of the well-known Russian actor Mosjukhin. We chose close-ups which were static and which did not express any feeling at all – quiet close-ups. We joined these close-ups, which were all similar, with other bits of film in three different combinations.

In the first combination the close-up of Mosjukhin was looking at the soup. In the second combination the face of Mosjukhin was joined in shots showing a coffin in which lay a dead woman. In the third the close-up was followed by a shot of a little girl playing with a funny toy bear. When we showed the three combinations to an audience which had not been let into the secret the result was terrific. The public raved about the acting of the artist. They pointed out the heavy pensiveness of his mood over the forgotten soup, were touched and moved by the deep sorrow which looked on the dead woman, and admired the light, happy smile with which he surveyed the girl at play. But we knew that in all three cases the face was exactly the same.
'Film Technique and Film Acting'
V.I. Pudovkin.

A classic example is one of the final shots in 'Citizen Kane' where a sledge with the word 'Rosebud' is thrown into a furnace. This information about the sledge attempts to link Kane's life and times. Another example occurs in 'The Third Man' where Joseph Cotton is in Vienna attempting to discover how his friend Harry Lime died. While he is looking out of an upstairs window on to a dark Vienna street a neighbour opens a shutter and a shaft of light strikes a dark doorway across the street to reveal Harry Lime in the shadows.

These examples relate to key images in the whole film but the same effect occurs within sections of a production. The significance of a scene can be signalled to the audience by a brief reaction close-up.

Objectivity

There is frequently a search for objectivity or neutrality in news or documentary coverage. The position a camera is located to observe an event is the result of a decision by the cameraman (or others) and, as such, it is part of the subjective judgement about the nature of the event. Frequently, as in the case of civil disturbances, the cameraman finds himself behind a line of police or army and his shots of stone-throwing protesters aimed apparently at the camera also subjectively threaten the viewer. There can be very little empathy for a line of violent agitated people advancing towards the lens. Reversing the camera position and placing it behind the protesters can also reverse subjective sympathy. Now the lens and the viewer is faced with a well-armed disciplined force that is bearing down on the viewer intent on breaking up the protest with force.

Violent events such as street disturbances allow the cameramen no discretion on his camera position. He has his own safety to safeguard as well as the practicalities of moving in a strife-torn and rapidly changing milieu. A balance may be attempted with the voice-over or piece to camera that accompanies such events but the force and the impact of the images often out-weigh any attempt at verbal balance or explanation.

The neutral news information shot is therefore extremely difficult to provide unless there is full knowledge of what the causes of the event are. This is usually only obtained after the event and hindsight is no help in topical newsgathering. Topicality requires a rapid response to the event and the urgent need to get the material back for the next available bulletin. The main consideration is to provide sufficient coverage for flexibility in editing to complement a voice-over updated report.

Multi-camera drama coverage

When the camera becomes interpretative rather than informative, the requirement is not simply that the screen acts as proscenium through which one observes staged events – a window to watch – it is rather that the total image produced is as important as the activity contained in that image. The shot becomes a symbol and can acquire a potency beyond the factual information it might contain. Clear visual communication requires good visual design to communicate clearly the intended message. The 'symbolic' image appears to have the ability to reach beyond the realism of the depicted scene and sum-up the meaning of the idea to be expressed in one powerful and direct image.

Image is a jargon word much loved by publicists and commercial makers. It is best described by example than by analysis, simply because the most arresting shots defy analysis and are justified only in the particular context in which they occur. An example from contemporary news coverage is the lone figure of a student facing an advancing tank in Tianemmen Square, Beijing. The shot is a brief factual record of a specific event but more significantly, it encapsulates the essence of any civil rights protest that is ruthlessly suppressed (see Figure 5.14).

That the image as a visual symbol occurs more often in film than in television is possibly the result of the conventions and working practices that grew up with the evolution of multi-camera technique in live television – a technique which is still retained even though its necessity has largely disappeared. There are obviously sound economic reasons for its survival and in some cases production advantages but the tenacity of its hold is also due to the persistence of convention and financial considerations.

It is often difficult to identify in any technique those limiting restraints which are imposed by the medium itself, and those restraints which exist through repetition. The re-valuation usually takes place when someone convincingly demonstrates that the old suppositions have been arbitrarily arrived at by producing a work which contradicts basic assumptions. An oft-quoted example is Orson Welles' film 'Citizen Kane' which, with a small number of innovations such as deep focus photography, ceiling sets, overlap sound and a narrative which folded back on itself in time, shifted current attitudes. Gregg Toland, his cinematographer, made this reply to criticism that the film contradicted essential camera technique:

I want to make a distinction between 'commandment' and 'convention'. Photographically speaking, I understand a commandment to be a rule, axiom, or principle, an incontrovertible fact of photographic procedure which is unchangeable for physical and chemical reasons. On the other hand, a convention to me, is a usage which has become acceptable through repetition. It is a tradition rather than a rule. With time the convention becomes a commandment, through force of habit. I feel the limiting effect is both obvious and unfortunate.

'How I Broke the Rules in "Citizen Kane"' Gregg Toland, *Popular Photography Magazine* 8 (June 1941).

Television camerawork tradition includes multi-camera shooting, rapid production techniques and continuous, impromptu framing adjustments. It may seem paradoxical to suggest that speed and flexibility may be just as rigid a convention as any dogmatic rule, but due to the need for a 'conveyor belt' production technique in programme making, productions continually rely on quick workable technique and reject or avoid innovation which may be time-consuming or unfamiliar. Speed of application is a convention and a necessity but frequently leads to shot compositions that have some 'rough edges' which have never been fully resolved, due to the shortage of rehearsal/recording time. This leads to camerawork that requires constant minor adjustments to the frame in order to accommodate actor position or staging that could have been re-plotted if time/budget (and the ever present need for multi-camera compromise) had been available.

The roots of this multi-camera tradition began with the constraints of live television. Live television had all the advantages of immediacy – as it happened so you saw it. Sport, quiz, discussion or drama were sliced up and presented by continuous camera coverage. Production techniques were pioneered, shaped and perfected to accommodate any event that could be staged in or out of a television studio. Lacking the ability to edit, every event dictated its own time scale. If a writhing footballer in a live match took two minutes to 'act out' that every bone in his body was broken, then every second of his agony was faithfully transmitted. Whilst a more legitimate actor in a multi-camera drama might benefit from a continuity of performance similar to his experience in the theatre, the cameraman's activity often reflected the tempo of the production varying from frantic haste to beat the cue light, to a leisurely pull out from the ringing phone to allow actors from the previous set to scuttle in under the lens, seat themselves and look, as they came into shot, as if they had been waiting for that particular phone call for hours. The premier advantage of television compared to film was that it reached an enormous number of people instantaneously. It was also cheaper. A ninety-minute play could, within two or three studio days, be rehearsed and transmitted at a fraction of the cost of a feature film. There was no point in comparing film with television, they were different animals. A live, ninety-minute play had a ninety-minute existence whereas a feature film had a commercial life to recover its financial and creative investment.

Live television drama was anchored to the clock. If an actor took ten paces to cross the set, then in some way that time duration would have to be accommodated by the camera coverage – six paces could not be clipped out and left on the cutting room floor. Time and space were the controlling factors for production staging and shooting. A number of shots had to be delivered from a variety of compromise positions. Time to get to the shot, time to deliver the shot, and time to reposition for the next shot were fixed by the time scale of the continuous event in front of the cameras. Because of the pressure of time and space many shots in live television were a poor compromise between what could be achieved and what was possible to achieve.

A cameraman framing a shot every ten or twenty seconds with a turret camera, on a set with a boom to his left and another camera to his right and six feet of floor space to call his own had little or no opportunity of avoiding an occasional 'CU face with distracting background'. Inconsequential background and poor compositional elements are almost inevitable at some stage of multi-camera shooting. An artiste's position may be perfect for one camera but produce an awkward framing for another. A slight re-positioning and a third shot was jeopardized. The eventual solution might have been satisfactory if not ideal. Although many productions were extremely successful, at its worst live TV drama could deteriorate into a logistics exercise in marshalling equipment and artiste; a triumph of reflex skills and coordinated expertise but failing to produce images that were an essential part of the production. Often the camera simply observed what was put in front of it rather than shaping and contributing. In this role, the electronic camera was relegated to a mechanical recording device with as little effect on the content as the telephone system has on a subscriber's conversation.

The 'snatch and grab' tempo demanded by this type of camera operation was not radically altered by the introduction of VTR and the development of tape editing. Recording breaks at first were taken simply to facilitate set, costume and make-up changes and to avoid the worst of the cavalry charges of artiste and equipment between sets. But the potential of stopping the clock and liberating the production from the confines of 'actuality' was soon realized.

Scripts could be submitted and produced which would have been impossible in a live situation. EdiTec, and later time-code editing, allowed any fluff, gaff or booboo to be removed without the time consuming process of re-recording whole sections before a butt joint point could be reached. (To the everlasting gratitude of sit-com audiences who, if they laughed on the first take, would be regarding the frantic floor manager with sullen hostility by the fourth.)

But corrective editing was not the biggest gain. The portable camera/recorder allowed the same flexibility of application as a film unit with even greater opportunities in image manipulation in post-production. Drama continued to be shot on video especially in the hugely popular genre of the twice/thrice weekly 'soap' series. Discontinuous recording and single-shot takes should have released multi-camera shooting from the compromise of 'live' technique. But the full advantage of this potential is inhibited by cost, experience and convention.

Cost is the most restrictive factor in the transition from quickly producing large chunks of usable television direct from a studio, to a method of production which involves both an extended studio production period and an extensive post-production period. Television has an insatiable appetite for new programmes and with a history of rapid production techniques it was unlikely that any innovation that increased costs would achieve immediate acceptance. Television studios were designed and equipped to produce a finished product – a 'live' transmission. Although many programmes are discontinuously recorded, the mechanics of production are conditioned by a capital investment in a technique that has been superseded. Lightweight location drama has neatly side-stepped this tradition and developed its own innovations, its expansion powered not only by the impetus of financial savings but by the results it has achieved.

The other influential factor on multi-camera drama was the popularity of storylines, settings and performances rooted in realism. The style of lighting and camerawork in mass audience television drama reflect this emphasis on realism and 'picture factory' production line utilizing multi-camera shooting echoes the same 'real time' shot structure treatment used on actuality events such as sport or state occasions. For many years, the same camera crews would be used on every type of television production and it was inevitable that they would employ similar techniques on all genres of programme formats.

Obviously there is a part of television which is live or rooted in live technique. Some actuality events such as sport or public events have their own sacrosanct time scale and capitalize on television's ability to transmit instantaneous pictures. There are also those programmes which are simply communicating information and require an unobtrusive technique free from interpretation. Obtrusive technique is usually grabbed by productions seeking 'spontaneity' – pop, quiz and entertainment productions that flash the viewer with multi-mixermotosis in an attempt to communicate in perpetual motion that it's all happening here and now.

There appears to be a different audience expectation between a 'film' and a 'play'. Whereas a cinema production is called a 'film' even though it is often made for, and by television companies, the video equivalent is often called a play. Single plays have gone out of favour with television audiences and most drama productions are either filmed or form part of a video soap series.

The single play on television had been related to the theatre and began simply as a recording of a theatre production. Even when the form developed, it appeared as if the camera were still anchored to the role of observing actors delivering dialogue. The gap between film and multi-camera production is caused by time and space constraints. As we have seen, time can be manipulated by single/camera single shot working but full advantage is not taken because of the expected higher ratio of recorded material expected from a studio compared to a film unit. Video production is seen as, and is required to be, much more productive than film production. Single camera/single shot video drama can use the same techniques but frequently (usually due to budget) the most popular video drama on UK television (soaps) are often shot in a multi-camera convention even if sometimes only a single camera is used.

The criticism that electronically generated pictures are unsubtle and scrappy has a basis of truth. Too many shots occur that are expedient rather than essential – mass produced and instantly forget-table. Built into the television system is a back-log of technique which has evolved to meet a condition which is no longer a prime consideration – namely that all productions have to be transmitted live.

Multi-camera records real time. Every action by the actor is recorded. This often results in superfluous movement being left in, otherwise the production process would gravitate to single shot/single take and lose its economic advantage of speed. Single camera/single shot has an entirely different feel to it. Time and space can be manipulated in many different ways to provide a flow of images that defy location and time continuity.

The development of drama television camerawork in the UK has been influenced by technology, cost and the structure of broadcast-ing. Live drama was enormously popular in the late 1950s/early 1960s and often achieved the highest audience viewing figures. More people watched drama on television and film than at any time in human history. One transmission of 'Romeo and Juliet' could be watched by more people than the entire population of England in Shakespeare's time.

Live drama was a prisoner to narrative time, studio floor space and the need for a constant flow of productions. A modified technique was developed when tape recording and greater post-production capability became available. The introduction of the lightweight television camera/recorder allowed video drama (if it could command the budgets) the same range and versatility as film although the single camera/single shot video production was often seen as 'cheap' film. Another development was a multi-camera technique where each camera's output was recorded alongside a pre-planned 'master' shot structure. With this technique, more latitude in the edit points and alternative shots can be selected in the post-production stage even though there is an increased pressure on the cameramen to keep a continuously usable picture when iso recorded.

Drama (television or film) is the most popular form of mass enter-tainment and whereas in the past, American companies dominated production and world distribution, the top UK TV ratings positions are now consistently monopolized by UK produced soaps. Video drama has inherited the mass produced industrial process of provid-ing for a 24-hour television service. As the number of distribution outlets has increased, audiences have fragmented and pressure on budgets has increased to provide cheaper programmes for smaller audiences. Once the conventions had been set by live coverage, electronic studio based drama found it very difficult to break clear of low budgets and few studio production days. If the director is away from the recording area (e.g. in a control room or scanner) there is also the breakdown of consultation and discussion about shots and the production process takes on the atmosphere of a 'picture factory'. There is also an easy availability of alternative shots in multi-camera shooting and this allows, at no cost, an avalanche of shots.

The effect on video camerawork of smaller budgets and a tradi-tion of 'cheap and quick' technique compared to film is that frequently shot structure is expedient rather than optimum. This often results in staging action for two or more cameras to save time on separate set-ups. Shots are often continued past the point where a cut would occur in the film which results in fidgety reframing by the use of zoom or track to accommodate additional artistes entering or leaving shot. This adjustment of frame (although often expertly disguised) is a common occurrence in video camerawork probably because the director is constantly monitoring the shot and is prepared to trade-off a less then satisfactory framing against the cost and time of another set-up.

Multi-camera shooting appears to encourage a convention of complicated stagings which require small 'zooms' and 'tidy-up' camera movement to keep a reasonable frame. This can be instantly achieved in a television studio because of smooth floors and cameras mounted on pedestals unlike feature film production where more deliberation and time is needed if a change of camera movement is required. Television drama often favours the two-person or three-person shot with people edging into small areas of frame. The camera is employed simply to provide pictures of actors exchanging dialogue. Multi-camera shooting provides a director with an instantly available wide range of shots. This in practice can deteriorate into a choice of shots covering a number of average and sometimes indifferent groupings and staging.

The major advantage of multi-camera television drama, however, is that it reaches a much larger audience than film but at a much lower cost. The lower revenue inevitably affects production time and production values. Film has a longer shelf life and is usually a self-contained item (apart from the surrounding merchandise). Television drama camerawork is just one facet of a continuous flow of programme output. Working against a punishing recording schedule, some programmes which seem short on production values in reality take an enormous application of skilful technique. Speed of application of television drama camerawork is an asset as well as being a liability.

Dance and composition

As in every type of production, there are many ways of covering dance on film and television. There are tried and trusted basic conventions and there are innovations and visual experiments that reject and oppose the following generalizations about dance composition. As was said in another context, an orgy of self-expression can sometimes be no more productive that the blind obedience to rules. The following observations are offered as a basis for development.

Dance features the whole figure and therefore the majority of shots will include the whole figure. The dance 'shape' can be emphasized by keeping the camera low and therefore reducing the amount of floor in shot and emphasizing the figure in relationship to the backing.

Let the dancers move within the frame. Be wide enough for the dancers to make their own shapes within the frame. Avoid constant panning to keep the dancer within the frame. The fidgety background will work against the dancer's movement and keeping the dancer in centre frame while they are moving can work against the intentions of the choreographer.

If the dance movement is interpreted by camera movement, there could be a confusion of choreographic design unless there is collaboration with the choreographer. Spins and twirls can be extended by mixing between shots which enhances the intended movement of the dancer. If possible, let the dancer choreograph to the frame. Show them the amount of studio floor space in shot and let the choreographer work out how they can best use this space.

Use a low-angle camera if the dancers are moving across frame. Use a high-angled camera if they are moving away or towards camera. Use a wide-angle to enhance speed of movement to and from camera. Use a narrow-angle to collapse space and movement. Use a close-up cut-in to disclose details of movement, to increase or express excitement in the dance. Devise shot-size to allow cuts on movement and music.

Summary

One aspect of the composition of a shot is to consider how it will relate to the preceding and succeeding shots. There must be a reason in editing to change shot and the cameraman has to provide a diversity of material to provide a cutting point. Edit-point requirements such as change in angle and shot size, subject movement, camera movement and continuity have to be considered and provided for to enable the footage to be assembled in a coherent stream of images. Shooting with editing in mind is therefore essential. It is part of the cameraman's craft to provide the editor/presenter with a variety of options but to keep the shooting ratio in proportion to the editing time available.

The narrative 'weight' of a shot is dependent on the size of the shot and also on the composition. Emphasis can be strengthened or lightened depending on the reason for the shot.

A good cut needs a change in shot size or significant change in content to be invisible.

12
Compositing

Compositing

Since the advent of digital post-production work, compositing has become the umbrella description of one of the oldest techniques in film production, namely, the combining of two or more separate images into one unified image. The intention of the techniques employed is to eliminate any indication in the final composite image of the join between the separate images that have been combined.

George Melies 'trick' films at the end of nineteenth century, made use of superimposition by winding back the film in the camera and making a second exposure. This early deployment of a composite shot highlighted the first essential requirement for combining two images – the need for perfect registration. Due to the imperfect registration of the early cameras, a second exposure through the camera resulted in the combined static images moving independently of each other. This shift of position exposed their separate nature.

Norman Dawn made one of the first glass shots in 1914 by making additions to the scene being photographed. Roofs were painted on a sheet of glass positioned several feet in front of the camera and positioned in scale and alignment with actual building (see *Film Style and Technique* by Barry Salt). This involved the second essential rule for composite shots – the accurate match of size, perspective, position, tone and shadow disposition when compositing two images (Figure 12.1).

To avoid the time-consuming business of actually painting the scene at the location with the locked off camera set up, Dawn later pioneered a glass matte shot which involved blacking out the unwanted part of the scene, shooting the action and then using a test strip of film taken at the same time, painting in the black area the required scenic additions before blacking out the rest of the shot. The painted footage was then exposed on the original shot.

Refinements of the matte technique were developed over the years as was the practice of building miniatures such as model scenery positioned close to the camera to overlay the main set. A famous example was in Ben Hur (1924) where a model of the top

Figure 12.1 Early glass shot technique (c. 1914) (a) The unwanted part of the scene is blacked out on the glass frame and the action is shot. After the action is shot another section of footage is exposed as a guide to the matte line for the additional painted scenic item. (b) The test footage is threaded into a camera and a light projected through the camera of a single frame focused onto an easel. The required additional scenic elements are painted onto the caption. (c) When this is complete, the area where the action takes place is blacked out. (d) The original negative is now loaded into the camera and exposed to the easel painting combining the art work action and the painted scenic elements.

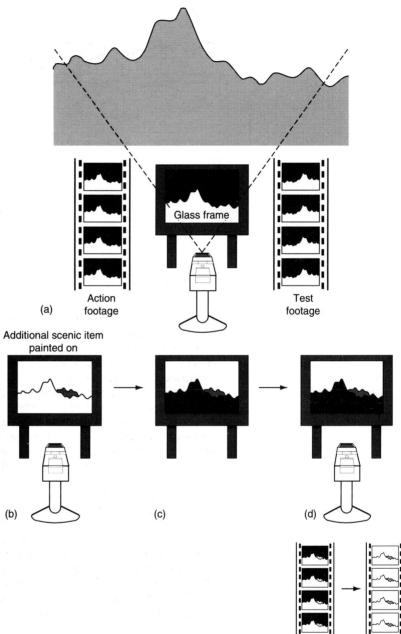

section of the amphitheatre was positioned to increase the scale and impact of the arena. In the mid-1920s, the Williams process allowed travelling mattes to combine a moving actor with a moving background and it has been suggested that this involved the early use of rotoscoping – projecting frame by frame in order to clean up or insert detail into each frame to produce a convincing composite.

The expansion of television production allowed the development of electronic keying by first using a luminance key (off-black or white) and then by colour separation – chroma keying using a saturated colour usually blue. Later variants such as linear keying allowed realistic semi-transparent effects such as transparent shadows and partial reflections.

The growth of digital post-production allowed enormous flexibility in re-arranging, combining and manipulating the structure of an image. Modern techniques allow digital keying, matting, painting, retouching, rotoscoping, image repair of keying and the combining of real and computer generated backgrounds.

In all these techniques, a 'seamless' product is the target. The aim is an invisible join between two or more images.

Electronic keying

Combining two images requires a switch to be inserted in the signal chain which will electronically select the appropriate image. Blue is commonly chosen as the colour to be used as the separation key but other colours can be employed. When the chroma key switch is in use, any blue in the selected image (foreground) is switched out and that part of the frame which contained a blue object is blanked. The black holes left in the shot are now used as a stencil to cut out the corresponding portions in the frame of the background image. The parts of the background image that are within this template are inserted (as a perfect fit) back into the blank areas of the foreground image (Figure 12.2).

Linear keying is similar to a film travelling matte system and does not switch between foreground and background. It suppresses the unwanted colour of the foreground (e.g. blue) and turns on the background image in proportion (linearly) to the brightness of the blue of the foreground image. Shadows cast by foreground objects can therefore be semi-transparent rather than black silhouettes.

Invisible keying of one image into another requires the application of a perfect electronic switch obtained by appropriate lighting of foreground and background, correct setting up and operation of the keying equipment, a match between foreground and background mood and atmosphere which is achieved by lighting and design, appropriate costume and make-up of foreground artists, a match between foreground artist's size, position and movement and background perspective achieved by camera position, lens and staging.

The following pages will centre on compositional techniques to achieve a match between foreground artist's size, position, movement and background perspective and staging for live action that can be employed to persuade the viewer that no technique has been employed.

Two-dimensional background

The simplest type of chroma or linear key camerawork is placing a presenter beside a primary colour panel and keying in a logo or a diagram such as a weather chart. As the infill image only exists in two dimensions, there is no problem with matching the perspective of the presenter (foreground) with the perspective of the keyed-in

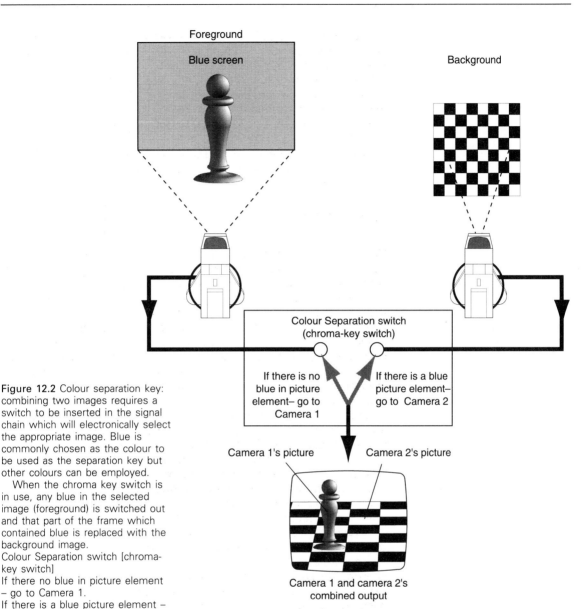

Figure 12.2 Colour separation key: combining two images requires a switch to be inserted in the signal chain which will electronically select the appropriate image. Blue is commonly chosen as the colour to be used as the separation key but other colours can be employed.

When the chroma key switch is in use, any blue in the selected image (foreground) is switched out and that part of the frame which contained blue is replaced with the background image.

Colour Separation switch [chroma-key switch]
If there no blue in picture element – go to Camera 1.
If there is a blue picture element – go to Camera 2.

image (background). The foreground camera will shoot all or part of the blue screen and any person or object placed in front of the screen will overlap or be 'in front' of the image that is keyed into the panel. The background weather chart can be generated by another camera simultaneously with the foreground camera. Combining the two images simply involves the foreground camera adjusting the framing to contain any artist movement. The background camera then adjusts its framing so that the required information fits the keyed area in the foreground shot.

Obviously, once this match has been achieved, neither camera can move without revealing that what appears to be a single image is in fact a composite of two different shots. In fact it is more probable that the weather chart will have been generated by computer graphics and keyed into the blue screen 'window' direct.

Any visual source – camera, frame store, computer graphics, VTR, film can be used for a key background and the image can be moving or static. The production intention with this type of composite is to persuade the viewer that the presenter is standing beside the weather chart and can point and touch any relevant part of it.

In fact as the presenter is simply looking at a blue screen there is a need for a monitor in their eye-line to guide them in their presentation. Another technique is to feed the composite picture to a prompt device on the camera they are talking to so that they can still gesture whilst talking to the viewer but have a mirror of themselves and the chart. A third solution is to stand the weatherman against a blue, back-lit screen which provides the keying colour whilst at the same time back projecting a faint image of the chart onto the screen. The forecaster can then actually see an image of the chart he is talking about.

Matching perspective of line and mass

The problems associated with keying a two-dimensional graphic into a picture are fairly straight forward compared to trying to achieve a realistic composite of two separate images. A pre-recorded background is often used either because of lack of floor space or lack of budget.

A typical example of compositing occurred in a production based on the life of a politician. The story required the statesman at one point to be in a deserted House of Commons. Because of the width of shot required, it would have been too expensive to build a replica of the Commons so therefore a recording of the Commons interior was made and then keyed into the blue screen in front of which the actor made the required movement.

The composite image combined the space recorded by the location camera with the space occupied by the actor in the studio. The

Figure 12.3 (a) Background subject; (b) foreground subject against blue screen; (c) the combined background and foreground; (d) camera height on foreground subject is too low; (e) camera height on foreground subject is too high.

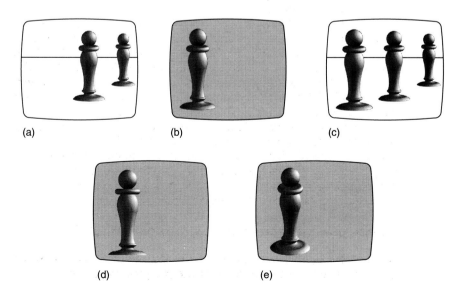

(a)   (b)   (c)

(d)   (e)

problem is to get the actor's studio space to be identical to the location space. If the resultant composite seeks to convince the viewer that both background and foreground are contiguous – that is, that they are adjacent and are observed from the same viewpoint, then the line perspective of both images will have to match in every particular. It is in matching the line and mass perspective of two images, especially if the background is pre-recorded and not subject to adjustment, that often cause the most problems in shooting on blue screen (Figures 12.3a–12.3e).

The problem is exacerbated if there is actor movement towards or away from the foreground camera. If the match is incorrect then it appears as if he inhabits a different space from his background. Which of course in reality is the case. Matching line perspective and the perspective of mass is the essential requirement for a seamless join between the foreground and background image.

Camera height, lens-angle and camera distance

As we discussed in the chapter on perspective, one of the perceptual methods we use to determine depth is to assess the rate by which objects appear to diminish/increase in size as they recede/approach us and the appearance of parallel lines that converge and vanish at the horizon.

Other depth indicators are atmospheric or aerial perspective. This is the optical effect of light being absorbed by mist, dust or moisture causing colours to become de-saturated and bluer and a reduction of contrast between tones the greater the distance from the observer. Binocular vision allows depth to be assessed by contrasting the two viewpoints of our eyes. This form of depth calculation is obviously not available in a two-dimensional image but overlap of objects is and gives clues to relative distance.

When a camera converts a three-dimensional scene into a TV picture, it leaves an imprint of lens height, camera tilt, distance from subject and lens-angle.

We can detect these decisions in any image by examining the position of the horizon line and where it cuts similar sized figures. This will reveal camera height and tilt. Lens-height and tilt will be revealed by any parallel converging lines in the image such as the edges of buildings or roads. The size relationship between foreground and background objects, particularly the human figure will gives clues to camera distance from objects and lens-angle. Camera distance from subject will be revealed by the change in object size when moving towards or away from the lens.

For any specific lens-angle and camera position there will be a unique set of the above parameters. The internal 'perspective' of the picture is created by the focal length of the lens except, of course, where false perspective has been deliberately created.

Planning a blue screen set-up (camera static)

Before setting out to achieve a composite shot the following questions need to be considered at the pre-planning stage.

1   What foreground actor movement will there be and how does this match with the background image?
2   If the action is towards or away from the camera, how will composition be affected if the foreground camera is unable to reframe?
3   Can the lens height of the foreground camera, its lens-angle and distance from subject contain the action and does it match the background camera's lens-angle, height and position?

In nearly all cases it is essential to make decisions about the foreground action before recording the background unless foreground action is simple and static.

Background/foreground camera height

Our normal perceptual experience of someone of our own size moving on flat ground towards us is that the horizon line will always intersect behind them at eye level. We have to duplicate this condition in the studio when the horizon line will be a separate image to an actor moving towards the lens. We have to ensure that our everyday experience of a three-dimensional world is convincingly reproduced when three dimensions are recorded as two separate two-dimensional images and then combined (Figures 12.4a–12.4c).

In terms of a perspective match on blue screen, the lens axis height and tilt becomes as important in achieving an invisible join as the 'crossing the line' conventions of picture editing. A jump cut across the line will register just as the wrong lens height may show up when actor movement is involved.

If the lens height of the level background camera was at eye-level, say 1.5 metres, then everyone in the foreground studio shot needs to be intersected at eye-level by the keyed or matted horizon line so they may move naturally towards and away from the camera.

Their position in the frame, relative to the background horizon line, follows our normal expectations of people walking on level ground. They must appear to grow progressively larger commiserate with their walking speed and their head must stay in the same relation to background horizon line. It must follow the horizontally parallel line from our eye (the lens) to the horizon. They must not cross the line.

If the foreground camera lens is higher than the background lens then a figure moving towards the camera will appear to be walking downhill and conflict with our expectations. Their head will start in frame above the line and the end of their movement will take their head below the line. This is identical with our perception of a person walking downhill even though the actor will be walking on a flat studio floor (Figures 12.5a–12.5c).

Likewise if the foreground camera is set too low then an approaching figure to camera will appear to be walking uphill. It is important to realize that it is not a differing lens-angle or subject distance that is causing this mismatch but lens height. Tracking the camera in or out, zooming in or out or tilting will not improve the perspective match until the foreground camera is at the same height as the camera that recorded the horizon.

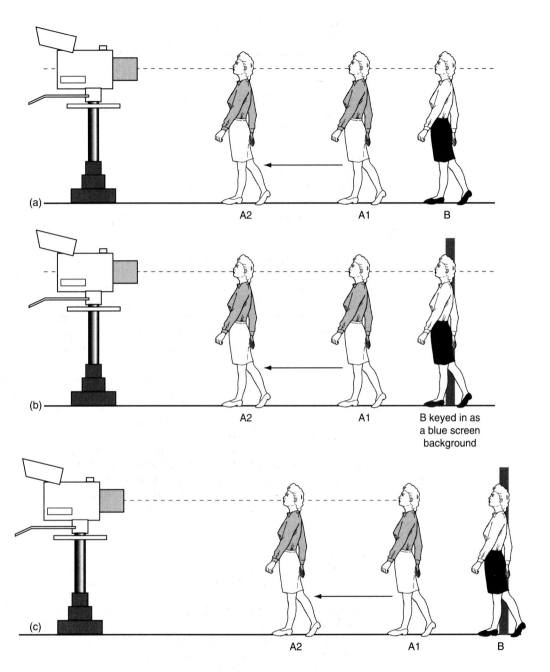

Figure 12.4 Matching camera to subject distance and lens-angle.
(a) With camera height at eye level, figure A walks towards the camera on level ground and grows progressively larger. (b) The same shot is now recreated on blue screen with B as the background and A walking towards the lens on blue. For the same change in size and height relationship in frame as in (a), the foreground camera has to duplicate the same height, subject distance, camera tilt and lens-angle as in (a). (c) If the foreground camera distance is greater than the background camera distance and image size is compensated by a smaller lens-angle, then the rate of A's walk will not match B's background space. Similarly, if the foreground camera distance to A is too close there will be a mismatch in A's walking speed and distance covered.

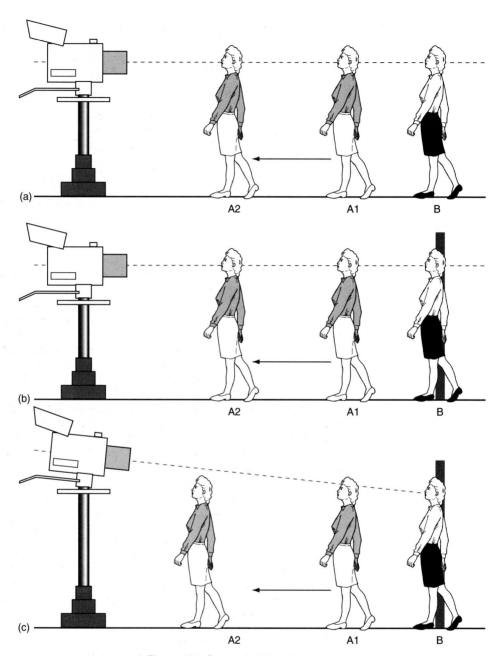

Figure 12.5 Camera height and blue screen.
(a) With level camera and lens at eye-height, person A, walking to camera on level ground, will always have their eyes at the same height in the frame as person B (assuming A and B are of the same height). (b) The same shot is now duplicated on blue screen with A on the foreground camera and B is keyed into the background. If the foreground camera's height, lens tilt, subject distance and lens-angle matches the background camera, A's walk will be appropriate to the space depicted in the keyed-in background. (c) The same blue screen set-up as in Figure 12.5b but the foreground camera lens height is too high and therefore the height of the projected line between A and B changes during A's walk. This produces the impression that A is walking downhill. Her head moves progressively lower in the frame as she approaches the lens in relation to the position of B's head.

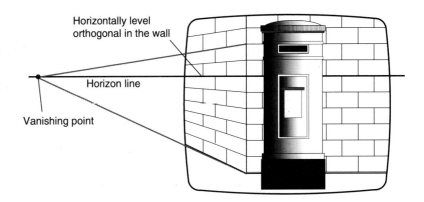

Figure 12.6 If the horizon line is not visible in the frame then projecting orthogonals back to where they meet at their vanishing point will establish the horizon. If there are no orthogonals, then parallel lines that are not square to the camera such as a brick wall may yield a horizontal line that will indicate the horizon line. Many cameras have a movable cursor in the viewfinder and this can be used to find the orthogonal that is horizontally level.

If we can find any object of standard height – post-box, farm-gate, table – and check where the horizon line intersects that object, that will indicate the lens height of the background camera.

Matching the unknown

For the reasons we have discussed, in nearly all cases it is essential to make decisions about the foreground action before recording the background. But what happens if you wish to match to an existing background that has not been specifically commissioned for a composite. Often, for the sake of economy or because the required location is not available or accessible or in 'season', a cameraman may find himself having to match to a background of which he has no information about lens height, angle or camera distance to subject.

The first parameter to decipher is the lens height of the background viewpoint so that you can match the lens height of the foreground camera. If the camera that recorded the background was level then it follows that the horizon line will bisect the frame. The strongest indicator of lens height is where the horizon line cuts a known height – usually the human figure.

If we can find any object of standard height – post-box, farm-gate, table, etc. – and check where the horizon line intersects that object, that will indicate the lens height of the background camera. If the horizon is centre frame and cuts a background figure at eye level then the foreground camera should be set to eye level.

If the horizon cuts at knee height then you require a lower foreground camera with the lens at this height. If the horizon line is not visible in frame then projecting orthogonals back to where they meet at their vanishing point will establish the horizon. If there are no orthogonals, then parallel lines that are not square to the camera such as a brick wall may yield a horizontal line that will indicate the horizon line. Most studio cameras have a movable cursor in the viewfinder and this can be used to find the orthogonal that is horizontally level (Figure 12.6).

If the background camera was tilted up or down then some detective work is required by the foreground cameraman. If the horizon line is in the top of the frame, then the background camera has tilted down. If it occurs in the lower half of the frame then the camera has taken the shot tilted up. Another indicator of tilt is the convergence of vertical lines. Just as orthogonals meet at a vanishing point, so do vertical parallel lines if not viewed at right-angles. Their meeting point is above or below the frame. An indication of the degree of background camera tilt will be gained from the degree of taper of

Figure 12.7 (a) Background
illustration for blue screen
sequence. (b) Boy walking against
blue screen following a line in the
studio that matches the drawn
path. (c) Combined picture.

(a)

(b)

(c)

Figure 12.8 A detail from 'The
Profanation of the Host' (1465),
Paolo Uccello.

vertical lines such as the parallel sides of buildings. But the devia-
tion of the lines from the vertical will also be affected by the distance
between the lines and the camera.

Just to recap on the linear perspective indicators of an image when
camera tilt and lens height are unknown.

1   Lens height equals the vanishing point of any orthogonals;
2   if there is a visible horizon with a level ground plane and it
    bisects the frame then the taking camera had no tilt;
3   if the vanishing point of orthogonals are below the horizon then
    the camera is tilted up; if the vanishing point is above the
    horizon then the camera is tilted down;
4   the lens height equals the height of the point where the horizon
    intersects similar sized objects (e.g. eye-height or waist-height,
    etc.);
5   if there are several equidistant orthogonals converging to a
    vanishing point, the orthogonal that is horizontal will indicate
    the position of the horizon. From this can be deduced lens height
    and tilt.

Working with illustrations

So far we have assumed the background image to be either a recording or a photographic still of a real location, but often illustrations
are used and these present their own set of problems (Figures 12.7a
and 12.7b).

The castle and its surrounding countryside is a perfectly convincing representation of a landscape. But keying the boy walking in this
'illustrated' space requires the boy to follow the drawn perspective.

In this case the illustration follows Alberti's laws of perspective and it is a matter of determining the lens height and lens-angle and staging the boy's walk so that it followed the drawn path. A speedy way of finding the path on the studio floor is to first determine the camera height. Then have a similar size stand-in positioned at the start of the walk and at the end of the walk to find camera distance. You will remember this determines size relationships. Then adjust the final overall framing with the zoom.

Calculating lens height and tilt

In Uccello's 'The Profanation of the Host' (see Figure 12.8), you will see the convergence of the line of tiles towards an horizon vanishing point beyond the end wall. Only one line between the tiles is vertical and that would occur from the artist's viewpoint in the centre of his field of view and therefore would be drawn in the centre of the painting.

This painting has more of a widescreen aspect ratio of 16:9 than the usual 4:3. The sides disappear when it is photographed for a 4×3 frame (unless we shoot off the top and bottom). If it is symmetrically cropped (i.e. an equal amount of painting on the left and the right is lost) then the vertical line of the tiles remains centre of frame. If, however, it was attempted to use the right-hand portion of the painting as a background and then walk someone through the doorway by using a matte on a blue background, the foreground camera could never match the background perspective. The horizontal tile lines would not appear parallel to the bottom of the frame unless the centre vertical join met the vanishing point in the centre of the horizon line. It would be impossible to match a foreground door into the background doorway and still have credible actor movement in foreground.

The important point to make with this example is to avoid asymmetrically cropping a background photograph or illustration because you may well end up creating an image with a linear perspective that cannot be replicated in the studio. Providing you zoom towards the centre of the photograph ensuring that you lose an equal amount of each border, you can get a tighter shot of the background and still preserve its linear perspective.

Masking and garbage mattes

It may not be necessary to use a large amount of blue screen backing to cover a very wide shot. There are many ways to disguise 'shoot off' such as a small foreground blue with a small aperture to reveal the foreground subject. Invisible wipes can be used through the vision mixer to mask unwanted areas of the image. Blue scenery pieces can be positioned to allow entrances and exits that are masked by elements in the background image and blue props can be used to walk on, sit or use as substitute for the image matted in.

Calculating lens-angle

Having found methods of detecting lens height and angle of camera tilt how would we go about deducing lens-angle and camera distance?

Looking at the 'Profanation of the Host' painting (see Figure 12.8), one can observe that Uccello has reduced the size of the tiles as they recede from the observer. The ratio of size change puzzled many painters until Alberti showed the common sense arithmetic of how the reduction in size is directly proportional to the distance from the eye.

A 1.5 metre man 2 metres from the lens will produce an image that is twice as large as a 1.5 metre man 4 metres from the camera (see Figure 3.10).

It is worth repeating that size relationships within the frame are the product of camera distance from the subject not the lens-angle. If a two shot was taken on a wide angle lens without *moving* the camera, and the same two people were taken on a narrow angle lens, their size relationship would be the same in both shots.

Confusion arises with this simple point because in attempting to match the foreground figure size on opposite ends of the zoom it is necessary to move the camera close to the subject in order to fill the frame when using the wide angle. It is the simple fact of moving the camera closer to the subject which changes the size relationship not the lens-angle.

The important point to remember is that subject size relationship is a product of camera distance. How the subject fills the frame is a product of lens-angle.

This, of course, is the crucial distinction between tracking and zooming. Tracking the camera towards or away from the subject alters size relationships – the perspective of mass. Zooming the lens, preserves the existing size relationships and magnifies or diminishes a portion of the shot.

The need to quote lens-angle v focal length

Foreground and background cameras should attempt to use the same lens-angle but this need not necessarily be the same focal length. Lens-angle or angle-of-view is related to the focal length of the lens and the *format size* of the pick-up sensor whether it be tube, chip or film gate. A 50 mm lens on a 35 mm stills camera will not produce the same angle of view as a 50 mm zoom lens setting on a Betacam. Whereas, the lens-angle of a 50 mm lens on a 16 mm film camera will match the 83 mm focal length setting on a 1.25" tube studio camera and provide similar perspective of mass assuming all other factors are equal.

Angle-of-view is therefore best stated in degrees rather than the dimension of the focal length of a lens when matching two different formats.

Calculating camera distance

We have seen that the distance from the lens to object will have an effect on perspective of mass and needs to be matched on background and foreground. How do we compute camera distance from a background visual?

If background and foreground are pre-planned then there is no problem. A foreground camera can duplicate the known background camera's lens and distance. But if we have to decode the angle of view of a recorded background or illustration then we need to use similar methods to the ones employed detecting camera height and tilt. In many ways the match is not so critical and there will only be a conflict between background and foreground image perspective of mass if it appears that the size of objects are changing at a non-uniform rate between chroma key backing and foreground.

Returning to the Uccello painting (see Figure 12.8), if this was used for a background and it was required to walk an actor from foreground up to the standing figure, we would need to compute the viewpoint distance of the painting and match that distance with the foreground camera. Using the rule that the decrease in size of an object is proportional to its distance from the eye, we could try to estimate the size decrease of the far side of the doorway with the near side.

Of course, it is only possible to use this method if we have two identical sized markers in a background and we know or can reasonably estimate the distance between them. The width of the tiles appear to be a quarter of the height of the figure. Therefore they could be approximately 40 cm square.

Fortunately, as Uccello had to calculate the very same distance that we are searching for when he painted the picture, he conveniently placed his downstage edge of the doorway on a tile join and the far edge on another tile join four tiles upstage. If we measure the height of the two ends of the doorway we find the upstage door frame about 3/4 the size of the downstage edge. Therefore as a decrease in size is proportional to distance, the far edge is 1 1/3 further away than the downstage edge.

Our viewpoint or rather Uccello when he painted the scene was just over 4 m from the edge of the downstage door frame. As the centre figure is standing on the same tile join as the downstage outer edge of the doorframe, an actor would need to be 4 m from the foreground camera when he was standing by the figure if he was required to walk in shot from camera.

His reduction in size and speed of movement over the painted tiles would then match the perspective of the painting. Confirmation of the correct foreground camera distance and lens-angle would be to check the foreground actors feet as he walks over the painted tiles. They are estimated to be 40 cm deep even though pictured foreshortened.

If he walks on the painted tiles with giant strides, then the camera is too close. Track out and zoom in. If he covers too little space for the length of his stride, then the camera is too far away. Track in and zoom out. If he floats across the painted tiles, then the camera is too high. Crane down and with this specific background that has a central horizon, level the camera. If his feet sink into the tiles, crane up and level up.

Camera movement

When a foreground artist is composited with a background image any camera movement by the foreground camera will displace the artist with relation to the background unless the camera providing the background image also duplicates the foreground movement, and visa versa.

Panning on the background image will 'fly' the foreground figure through space. To achieve natural movement of a combined image both foreground and background movement have to be in perfect synchronization. The synchronization must provide not only for the same ratio of change in picture size in background and foreground image but a perfect match in perspective change.

Synchronization of perspective change is therefore almost impossible to achieve with manually operated cameras but can be guaranteed with a motion control rig.

Motion rigs

A motion control rig is a camera mounted on a motorized crane where all movement of its lens in space is computer controlled. A timed series of camera movements on the first 'pass' is memorized by its controlling computer which can then provide an exact copy of the movement on a second 'pass' or subsequent recordings.

Memory heads

Precise duplication of movement of background and foreground images to ensure that the combined image stays in register during camera movement can also be achieved by using a pan-and-tilt head which records each movement on a computer disc.

The background scene can be pre-recorded using a memory head and all the essential data that we have talked about, namely lens height, lens-angle, tilt, distance from subject, speed of pan, tilt, zoom movement, speed of zoom and focus can be memorized on a floppy disc which can then be used to programme the foreground camera to duplicate camera moves on the foreground subject on blue. It can also be used to synchronize two camera movements so that there is no image slip between the composited shots.

Motion capture

One of the problems of computer generated images of people in motion is to depict accurately the complexity of the body movement. Motion capture is a technique where the movement and the positions of the limbs in real-time action is captured as motion data which can be transformed into computer generated three-dimensional animation. One method of motion capture involves attaching numerous sensors to the body at strategic places such as joints and limb extremities which relay for any specific thirty-second action, their continually changing position in space to a computer. Another method uses light reflectors attached to the body to relay positions in space.

Virtual studios

As the cost of computing power decreases, more and more facilities utilizing enormous amounts of computer memory are available for production. Virtual scene construction allows an artiste moving on a blue screen background to be composited into an electronically generated background based on a still or electronically created.

The foreground camera capturing the artiste on blue can pan, track and move with the subject and the computer software will automatically alter the background accordingly. The distance from camera to presenter is continuously calculated and fed to the computer. This allows them to appear to walk behind and in front of computer-generated graphic 'objects' (such as simulated furniture) which is composited into the shot.

The claim for the virtual reality studio is that it can exist simply as a blue screen studio whilst its keyed 'scenery' will be held in the computer to be changed, depending on programme format, at the touch of a button. The system allows more than one camera to be used and to be routed as normal through a mixing panel for intercutting. Each shot will have the appropriate section of the computer-generated set as background.

Differential focus and depth of field

A simple technique for creating depth on a composite sequence is differential focus. By throwing the background out of focus a better foreground to background match can be achieved. This simulates the depth of field that is normally available on close-ups. Throwing the background out of focus also helps for better edits using portions of the same illustration. Another point to bear in mind with depth of field is the need to create a believable focus-zone gradation between background and foreground. It might be necessary to pre-record the background slightly out of focus to match the foreground action depending on size of shot on foreground actor. An everyday example of this is the newsreader in front of blue with a keyed-in picture of a defocused newsroom.

Background problem compositions

If the foreground camera is limited in its framing by the restraints of matching both the linear perspective and mass perspective there are situations where a difficult or unacceptable framing arises.

A foreground figure will be either too high in the frame or too low and the camera is unable to tilt or crane to compensate because this will destroy the perspective match. Typically this happens if there is a high horizon and low lens height on the background camera and an artiste walks towards the foreground camera. The result is crushed headroom on foreground with no way of compensating.

The reverse produces the opposite problem. A low horizon and above eye-line lens height on the background camera will create excessive headroom in foreground as the subject moves towards camera. Little or nothing can be done by the foreground camera to provide a more acceptable framing. The solution lies in changing the background to fit the required foreground framing and/or restaging the foreground action. This may cause a serious problem that could be avoided by production pre-planning.

It is important to remember that the lens height, lens-angle, camera distance from subject and camera tilt of the camera recording the background will control and constrain any subsequent foreground movement on chroma key.

Summary

Invisible keying of one image into another requires the application of a perfect electronic switch obtained by appropriate lighting of foreground and background, correct setting up and operation of the keying equipment, a match between foreground and background mood and atmosphere achieved by lighting and design, appropriate costume and make-up of foreground artists, a match between foreground artist's size, position, movement and background perspective achieved by camera position, lens and staging.

Matching line perspective and the perspective of mass is the essential requirement for a seamless join between the foreground and background image. If the resultant composite seeks to convince the viewer that both background and foreground are contiguous – that is, that they are adjacent and are observed from the same viewpoint, then the line perspective of both images will have to match in every particular. Subject size relationship is a product of camera distance. How the subject fills the frame is a product of lens-angle. Camera height and tilt of foreground and background camera must match if there is to be realistic actor movement towards or away from the lens.

Endnote

It is natural, when training for a craft or a new skill, to search for underlying rules and guidelines – to look for certainties in order to master and to measure the amount of progress achieved.

Camerawork is basically a craft but with its top practitioners it shades into a highly original, creative activity. Between learning by rote and the wilder excesses of individual subjective expression, a balance has to be struck between the dogma of 'always do it this way' and the anarchy of 'I don't quite know what I am trying to achieve, but out of this creative muddle new, original work will materialize. I hope!'

This book has discussed the constituent parts of composition. From the theory of perception to the inherited values of previous 'visual problem' solvers there is a wide range of advice and opinion on how to achieve good communication. Composition is central to this process and touches nearly all aspects of film and television production. To rewrite Marshall McLuans's media catch-phrase – the image is frequently the message.

What has not been discussed so far, is the part played by individual innovation in the act of framing up a shot. The imaginative leap made in the early days of film making when cameramen and directors devised and invented new visual ways of telling a story has been continuously expanded and added to by many cameramen following in their footsteps.

The television pioneers faced similar challenges with the need to adapt and develop multi-camera technique. The unpredictability of the early electronic camera created a demand for reliability and certainty. The engineering quest was for equipment of high specification coupled with a cost-effective life before being superseded by the next innovation.

Cameramen also have a keen interest in reliable equipment but frequently need to add another ingredient to the mixture. Good camerawork, as well as requiring a technique that guarantees a quality product, also, at times, involves taking risks. There are occasions when no previous experience or guidelines can help in resolving a particular visual problem.

In live television camerawork, operational decisions have to be made in seconds. The cameraman chances his arm and goes with what he feels is the relevant action. If he is right, then the result on screen is so obvious, that a viewer is not even aware that a split-second decision has been made. If he is wrong, the same viewer may be critical of the blunder. These visual decisions are made in seconds. The critic of these activities frequently have days, weeks or even months to make their critical decisions – and they can still get them wrong!

Cameramen have to live with uncertainty. It is part of the job. The programme may not be as good as they hoped, the film does not quite come off, etc., but stepping into the unknown – risk taking – is part of the everyday activity faced by production crews. There can never be absolute certainties about TV and film production technique and frequently, the new and the original are resisted until they achieve critical or financial endorsement.

Innovation, original work, is often the product of maverick thinking. A particular craft technique continues to be practised until someone demonstrates that it is based on unexamined assumptions. There are other ways of doing it.

It may have been implied in this discussion on composition that there is a clear, unequivocal method of work, but the creative urge to experiment, to try something different is as valuable as the need to have knowledge about the bricks and mortar of camerawork. Usually, innovation only succeeds if it takes off from an established craft skill. Genius is a commodity that is always in short supply.

The ability to create interesting and arresting compositions lies at the heart of the cameraman's expertise. The range and variety of outstanding camerawork testifies to the individuality present in the practice of the craft of camerawork. It would seem presumptuous to attempt to lay out principles and guidelines that would embrace such a diversity of practice. Technique changes too rapidly to attempt to set a discussion on composition in 'tablets of stone'.

Perhaps an eminent writer on the subject, Sir Charles Holmes ('Notes on the Science of Picture Making'), should have the last word:

It cannot be too definitely stated at the outset that a knowledge of principles is no substitute for invention. Principles themselves cannot create a work of art. They can only modify and perfect the vague pictorial conception formed in the artist's mind, which are the foundation upon which he builds.

Bibliography

Arnheim, Rudolph, *Art and Visual Perception*. Faber & Faber, London, 1967

Barthes, Roland, *Mythologies*. Jonathan Cape, London, 1972

Crowther, Bruce, *Film Noir*. W.H. Allen & Co., London, 1988

Gombrich, E.H., *The Image and the Eye*. Phaidon Press, London, 1982

Gombrich, E.H., *Art and Illusion*. Phaidon Press, London, 1960

Holmes, Sir Charles, *Notes on the Science of Picture Making*.

Itten, Johannes, *The Art of Colour*. Reinhold, New York, 1962

Kepes, Gyorgy, *Language of Vision*. Paul Theobald & Co., Chicago, 1961

Pudovkin, V.I., *Film Technique and Film Acting*. Lear Publishing Inc., New York, 1939

Salt, Barry, *Film Style and Technology: History and Analysis*. Starword, London, 1983

Scharf, Aaron, *Art and Photography*. The Penguin Press, London, 1968

Vesey, Godfrey (ed), *Philosophy in the Open*. The Open University Press, Milton Keynes, 1974

Index